Biology

Preliminary & Trial Higher School Certificate Examination Practice Papers 2023 Edition

Cherine Spirou
& Bill Matchett
(Editors)

Five Senses Education Pty Ltd
2/195 Prospect Highway
Seven Hills 2147
New South Wales
Australia

Cherine Spirou & Bill Matchett (Editors)
LAZSTA (Metropolitan South West Science Teachers Association)
Biology Practice Papers 2023
ISBN 978-1-76032-596-1

Contents

2019 Trial Higher School Certificate Examination	**1**
Marking guidelines	19
2020 Preliminary Examination	**33**
Marking guidelines	51
Mapping grid	60
2020 Trial Higher School Certificate Examination	**63**
Marking guidelines	83
Mapping grid	96
2021 Preliminary Examination	**99**
Marking guidelines	117
Mapping grid	127
2021 Trial Higher School Certificate Examination	**129**
Marking guidelines	152
Mapping grid	168
2022 Preliminary Examination	**171**
Marking guidelines	192
Mapping grid	202
2022 Trial Higher School Certificate Examination	**205**
Marking guidelines	228
Mapping grid	245

Biology

Trial Higher School Certificate Examination

2019

General Instructions	• Reading Time – 5 minutes • Working Time – 3 hours • Write using black pen • Draw diagrams using pencil • NESA approved calculators may be used
Total Marks	**Section I – 20 marks (pages 31 – 37)** • Attempt questions 1 – 20 • Allow about 35 minutes for this section **Section II – 80 marks (pages 38 – 48)** • Attempt questions 21 – 35 • Allow about 2 hours and 35 minutes for this section

Section I – Multiple Choice
20 marks (1 mark each)
Please answer on the answer sheet provided

1. Both external and internal fertilisation has advantages for organisms during reproduction. Which of the choices below include an advantage for both external and internal fertilisation?

	Internal	**External**
A.	Usually slower process	Large numbers produced
B.	Less gametes need to be produced	Large numbers produced
C.	Higher change of fertilisation	Lower chance of fertilisation
D.	Finding a compatible mate	Gametes exposed to predation

2. How are somatic mutations different from germline mutations?

   A. Somatic mutations affect the gametes and be passed on to offspring, while germline only affect body cells.
   B. Somatic mutations are a result of DNA replication while germline mutations occur in DNA translation.
   C. Somatic mutations are a result of DNA translation while germline mutations occur in DNA replication.
   D. Somatic mutations affect body cells and are not passed on to offspring, while germline only affect gamete cells.

3. A chemical mutagen operates by:

   A. removing electrons from atoms causing ionisation.
   B. cause thymine or cytosine to cause adjacent bonds.
   C. becoming incorporated into the DNA and cause mispairing.
   D. insert sections of their genome into the host DNA.

4. The transmission of the infectious disease Malaria is facilitated by the female *Anopheles* mosquito. This is an example of transmission by:

   A. Direct Contact.
   B. Indirect Contact.
   C. Vector.
   D. Vaccination.

5. Which cells are responsible for the production of antibodies:

   A. Killer T cells
   B. Phagocytes
   C. Helper T cells
   D. Plasma Cells

6. Look at the information presented below about the incidence of type 2 diabetes in Australia in 2017:

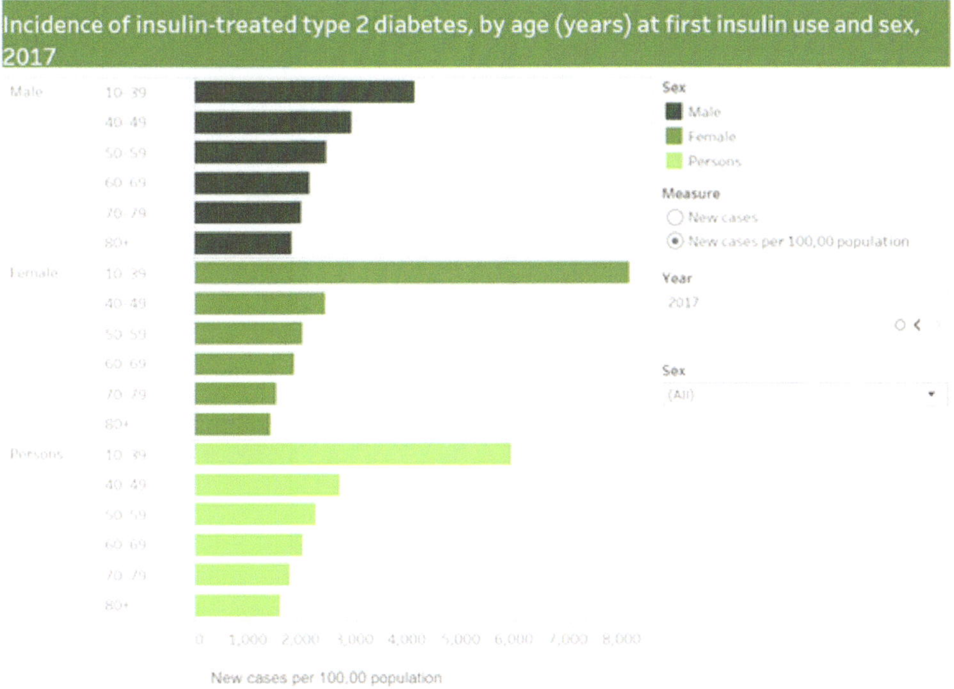

Source: Australian Institute of Health and Welfare

Which statement is correct based on the information presented in the graph?

A. More males contract insulin dependent diabetes than females

B. Diabetes is a non-infectious disease

C. Pregnant women are most at risk of contracting type 2 diabetes

D. Under the age of 40 more females contract type 2 diabetes than males

7.

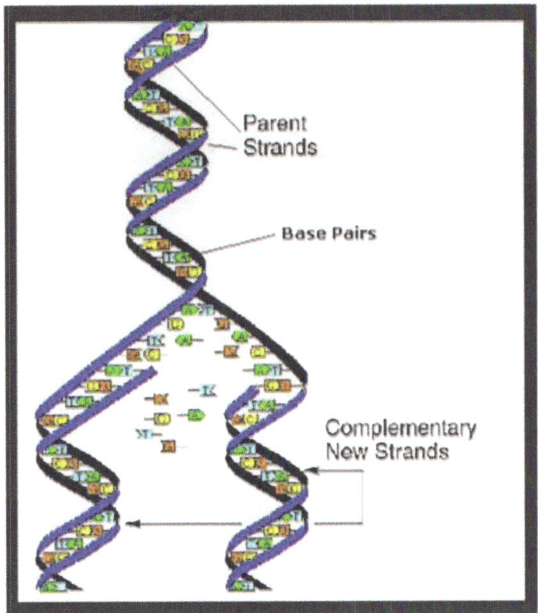

The above process illustrates:

A. Part of the adaptive immune system
B. A model of polypeptide synthesis
C. An essential process involved in cell division
D. A method used in forming transgenes

8. In Roses, a pure breeding Red rose can be crossed with a pure breeding white rose and all the offspring produced have pink flowers.

This is an example of:

A. Co-dominance
B. Incomplete dominance
C. Mutation
D. Mendalian Inheritance

9. The part of meiosis that is a **natural** example of recombinant DNA formation is

A. Crossing over between sister chromatids
B. The production of a transgenic species
C. Formation of haploid gametes
D. Crossing a horse with a donkey

10. Below is a sequence of events that can be used for creating a transgenic bacterium by "cutting and pasting".

Step 1 Recombinant DNA is formed by sealing the desired gene into the plasmid using DNA ligase enzyme
Step 2 The desired gene is "cut out" of an organism's DNA using a restriction enzyme
Step 3 Plasmid is removed from a bacterium and cut with a restriction enzyme
Step 4 The recombinant DNA plasmid is inserted into a bacterium - making it a transgenic bacterium

The correct order of the steps to create a transgenic bacterium is:

A. 2-3-4-1
B. 4-3-1-2
C. 3-2-4-1
D. 3-2-1-4

11. Below is a diagram showing the reproductive parts of a flower.

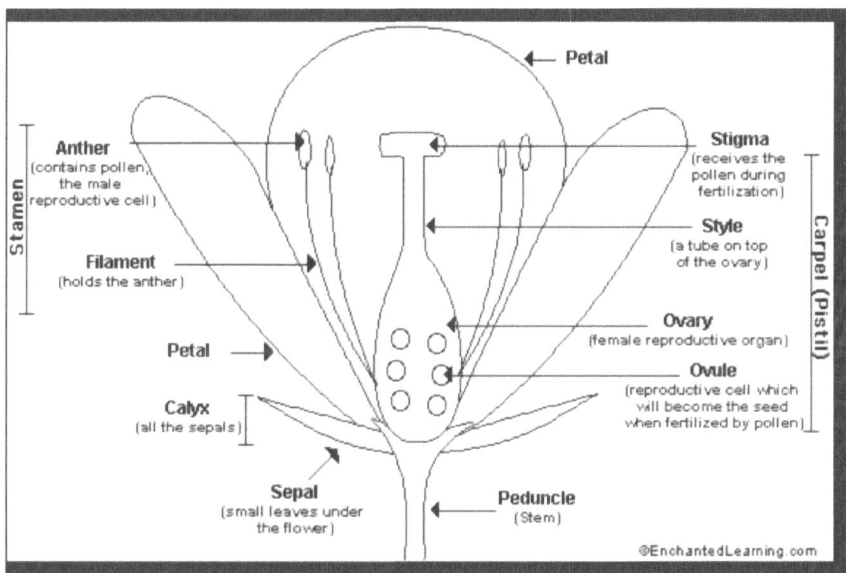

A backyard gardener wanted to artificially pollinate his only passion fruit vine growing in his backyard and he did this using a paint brush, gently moving from flower to flower transferring pollen from the anther to stigma on each flower.

Which statement is correct:

A. This is a form of asexual reproduction as the fruit produced will all be from the same plant
B. The gardener by doing this means the plant does no longer undergo meiosis
C. This is a form of sexual reproduction as it still involves the uniting of male and female gametes
D. This is a type of asexual reproduction as all the fruit produced will carry the same genetic makeup in their seeds.

12. A pathogen was identified as being heterotrophic, containing a cell wall, and was eukaryotic.

This pathogen is best described as a

A. Protozoan
B. Fungi
C. Bacteria
D. Prion

13. Vaccinations are given to people to help prevent certain diseases. They do this by

A. Stimulating the inflammatory response which destroys invading pathogens
B. Stimulating the bodies humoral immune system by producing specific antibodies, and activating B Memory cells
C. Destroy the invading pathogen directly
D. producing phagocytes which kill pathogens

14. Dialysis is a treatment for -

A. People who have myopia
B. Kidney failure
C. Hearing loss
D. Diabetes

15. Which of the following is a behavioural adaptation in humans in response to changing body temperature?

A. Presence of hair
B. Sweat glands in skin
C. Shivering
D. Moving into the shade to cool down

16. The diagram below shows a section of mRNA.

U-C-U-G-A

Which one of the following shows the base sequence on the template (or sense) strand of DNA from which this piece of mRNA was transcribed?

A. TGTCT
B. AGACU
C. TGTCU
D. AGACT

17. In Humans colour blindness is a sex-linked recessive condition carried on the X chromosome.

    If a colour–blind male has a son to a woman who has normal vision with no history of colour blindness in her family, what are the chances of their son being colour blind?

    A. 0%
    B. 50%
    C. 25%
    D. 100%

18. What is an antigen?

    A. Any foreign substances that causes an immune response.
    B. An invading microorganism.
    C. A membrane bound receptor.
    D. A modified white blood cell.

19. Homeostasis is

    A. a changing internal environment as a result of a changing external environment.
    B. a relatively stable internal environment as a result of a changing external environment.
    C. coordination between the nervous and endocrine system.
    D. a reflex response to a stimulus

20. Data has been collected over a number of years and analysed to establish a link between Lung Cancer and Smoking. This is an example of:

    A. An Hypothesis
    B. An Epidemiological Study
    C. A Postulate
    D. An Infectious Disease

End of Section I

Section II continued next page

Section II – Written responses
80 marks (2 – 9 marks)
Please write your answers in the spaces provided

Question 21 (3 marks)

The pedigree below shows the incidence of cystic fibrosis in a family. The CFTR gene in humans produces a transmembrane protein (the CFTR protein). This protein helps to control the movement of salts in and out of cells. It affects how fluid the mucous secretions are in the lungs.

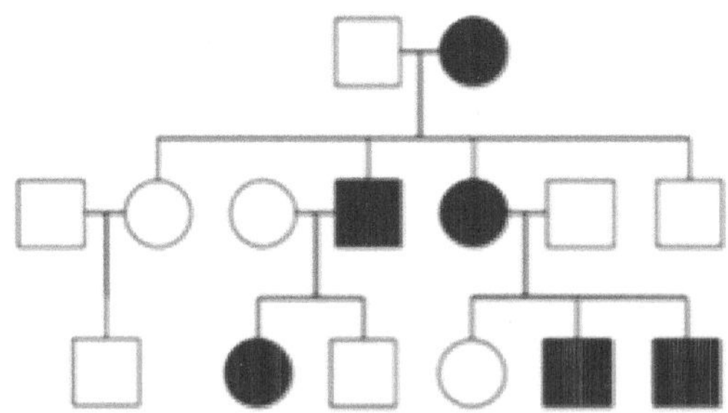

The lack of functional CFTR proteins causes cystic fibrosis, a recessively inherited, life threatening disease.

Explain how the use of family pedigrees be used to reduce the incidence of CF in a population?

....
....
....
....
....

Question 22 (5 marks)

The DNA sequence below shows the difference between those who suffer or don't suffer cystic fibrosis.

Dna sequence resulting in no cystic	Dna sequence resulting in cystic fibrosis
GGTATTGTT	GGTTTTGTT

(a) Identify the type of mutation shown in the diagram 1

....

(b) Beginning with DNA, construct a flow chart to show how this change in DNA would result in this dis-functional protein being produced. 4

Question 23 (6 marks)

Explain the contributions each of the scientists, Pasteur and Koch, made to our current understanding of infectious diseases. Discuss how their conclusions are used today to prevent the spread of disease.

....
....
....
....
....
....
....
....
....
....

Question 24 (5 marks)

The image below models a process that occurs during cell division.

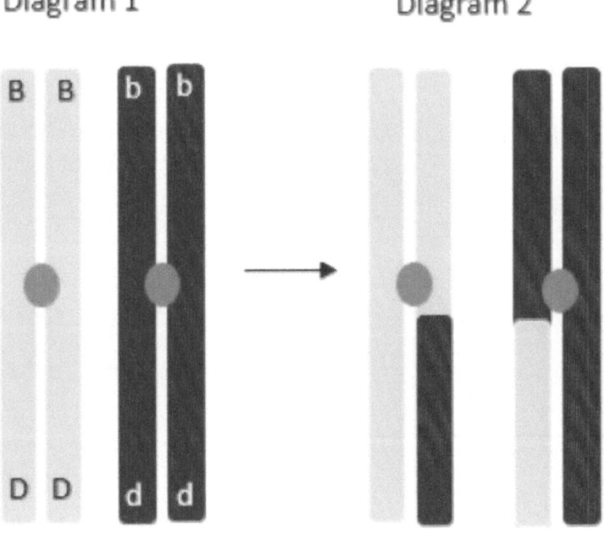

(a) On the diagram annotate the change in genotype as a result of this process. 1

(b) Describe the process shown in the diagram. 4

....
....
....
....

Question 25 (5 marks)

Draw an annotated negative feedback loop for the homeostatic control of temperature.

Question 26 (8 marks)

During your study of Module 7 you designed and conducted a practical investigation relating to the microbial testing of water or food samples.

(a) State the hypothesis for your investigation. 1

....

....

(b) Explain how you ensured your investigation was valid. 3

....

....

....

....

(c) Describe how you collected and presented your data. 4

....
....
....
....
....
....

Question 27 (9 marks)

READ THE ARTICLE BELOW ABOUT Bt COTTON

Bt crops have been produced by extracting genetic material from a bacterium, *Bacillus thuringiensis*, and inserting it into the DNA of various crop plants. The bacterial genes make the crop plants inedible to insect pests, greatly reducing the need for pesticides.

So far, Bt strains of cotton, maize, potatoes and several other commercially important crops have been developed.

The bacterium *Bacillus thuringiensis* was first discovered in 1901 and its toxic proteins were extracted and used as an insecticide in the 1920s.

The first genetically modified Bt plants, Bt cotton, were produced in 1985.

Problems with Bt use.

Insect pests typically evolve resistance to conventional pesticides and can be expected to eventually do the same with Bt crops

Sources: www.bio.davidson.edu and Wikepedia

(a) Identify the type of compound which is toxic to insects in Bt plants. 1

....

(b) Explain how insect pests might evolve a resistance to Bt. 2

....
....
....
....

(c) Assess the implications of the development of Bt crops for society and the environment. 4

....
....
....
....
....
....
....

(d) Explain why some people object to developments of this sort on ethical grounds. 2

....
....
....
....

Question 28 (4 marks)

Assess the effect of the cell replication processes on the continuity of species in both unicellular and multicellular organisms.

....
....
....
....
....
....
....
....
....
....
....
....
....
....

Question 29 (5 marks)

A group of students performed an experiment to investigate the growth of microorganisms in tea.

They set up 2 identical flasks with 200 mL of black tea in each. One flask was left open to the air and the other had some curved glass tubing. (See students diagram below)

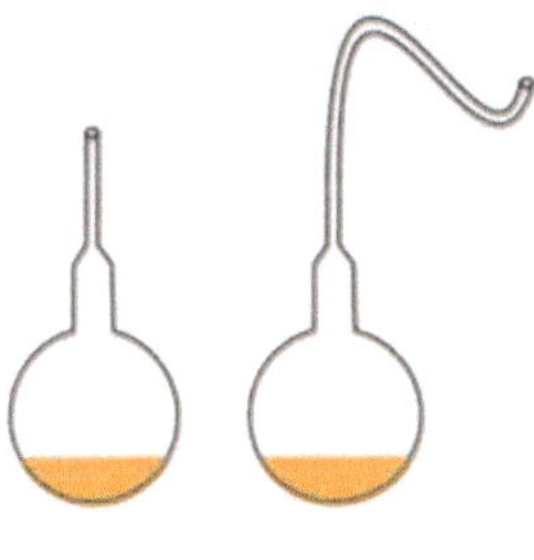

IMAGE COURTESY OF WILLIAM HARRIS

(a) Why did the students boil both flasks? 1

....

....

(b) Identify the independent and dependent variable in this investigation. 1

....

(c) How could the reliability of the experiment be improved? 1

....

....

(d) Explain the results the students obtained 2

....

....

....

....

Question 30 (7 marks)

(a) Compare DNA sequencing and DNA profiling. 3

....

....

....

....

(b) With reference to the diagram, determine the mostly likely father (1, 2 or 3) and justify your choice. 4

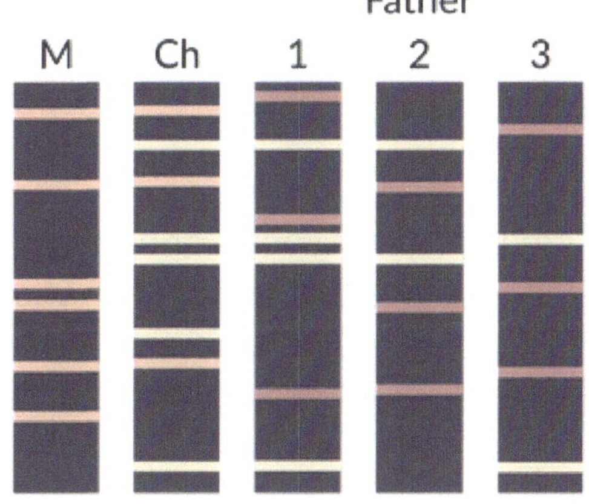

....

....

....

....

....

Question 31 (3 marks)

The Australian government funds a public health campaign offering free breast screening for breast cancer.

Explain the benefits of such a public health campaign to our society.

....
....
....
....
....

Question 32 (9 marks)

An outbreak of a disease has occurred in a preschool over a period of 4 days. Of the 40 children that attend, 20 have become ill and 5 of the 18 staff who work at the preschool have also fallen ill. All the patients have shown a reddish rash on their arms and some swelling in their joints. No family members of those that have the disease have shown any symptoms.

Design an epidemiological study to try and determine the cause of this disease.

....
....
....
....
....
....
....
....
....
....
....
....
....
....
....
....
....
....
....
....
....
....
....
....
....

Question 33 (7 marks)

The following diagram shows a form of technology used to overcome the disorder of hearing loss.

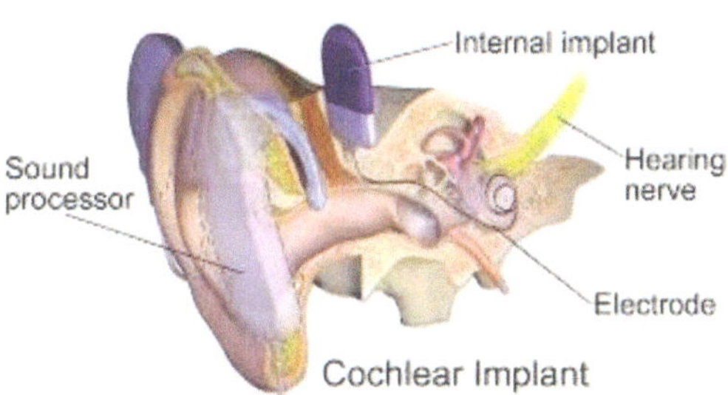

Cochlear Implant

(a) Describe how the cochlear implant overcomes the disorder of hearing loss in relation to the structure and function of the ear. 4

....
....
....
....
....
....
....
....

(b) Evaluate the effectiveness of the cochlear implant in managing hearing loss. 3

....
....
....
....
....
....
....
....

Question 34 (4 marks)

Using a named example, explain how population genetic data has been used in conservation management.

....
....
....
....
....
....
....
....

Question 35 (2 marks)

Pathogens have adaptations to assist in invading their host. Identify one such adaptation in a named pathogen and explain how it assists invasions.

....
....
....
....

End of Examination

LMC Biology Trial Marking Guidelines

Section I: Multiple-choice Answer Key

Question	Answer
1	B
2	D
3	C
4	C
5	D
6	D
7	C
8	B
9	A
10	D
11	C
12	B
13	B
14	B
15	D
16	D
17	A
18	A
19	B
20	B

Section II

Question 21

Criteria	Marks
States how pedigrees can • identify carriers in a family. • Be then used to predict the probability of those with the condition (or carriers) of giving birth to children with the disease • Indicates one way this can be used to reduce the incidence in a population	3
States how pedigrees can • identify carriers in a family. OR • Be then used to predict the probability of those with the condition (or carriers) of giving birth to children with the disease AND • Indicates one way this can be used to reduce the incidence in a population	2
• Mentions any piece of information pedigrees can show	1

Sample answer:
Pedigrees allow the identification of those members in the family who are sufferers and those who are carriers by using dominant and recessive alleles and homozygous and heterozygous genotypes. From this information Punnett squares can be used to determine the probabilities of carrier parents producing offspring that suffer from cystic fibrosis. Further prenatal testing could then be performed to confirm the presence of cystic fibrosis. This could be used to assist parents in making the decision to have or continue to have children.

Question 22 (a)

Criteria	Marks
Correct type, either Pont or Substitution	1

Sample answer:
Point mutation or base substitution

Question 22 (b)

Criteria	Marks
• Constructs a flow chart beginning with DNA • Includes a correct sequence of steps, showing the correct corresponding change in mRNA, and change in codons resulting in a change in an acid sequence, polypeptide chain and the resulting change in protein.	4
• Constructs a flow chart beginning with DNA • Includes a correct sequence of steps, showing the corresponding change in mRNA, **and/or** change in codons resulting in a change in an acid sequence, polypeptide chain and the resulting change in protein.	3
• Most steps included • Flow chart begins with DNA • Indicates a change in codon • Results in a change in protein OR • Flow chart begins with DNA • One correct step • Results in a change in protein	2
• Includes some relevant information about polypeptide synthesis	1

Sample answer:

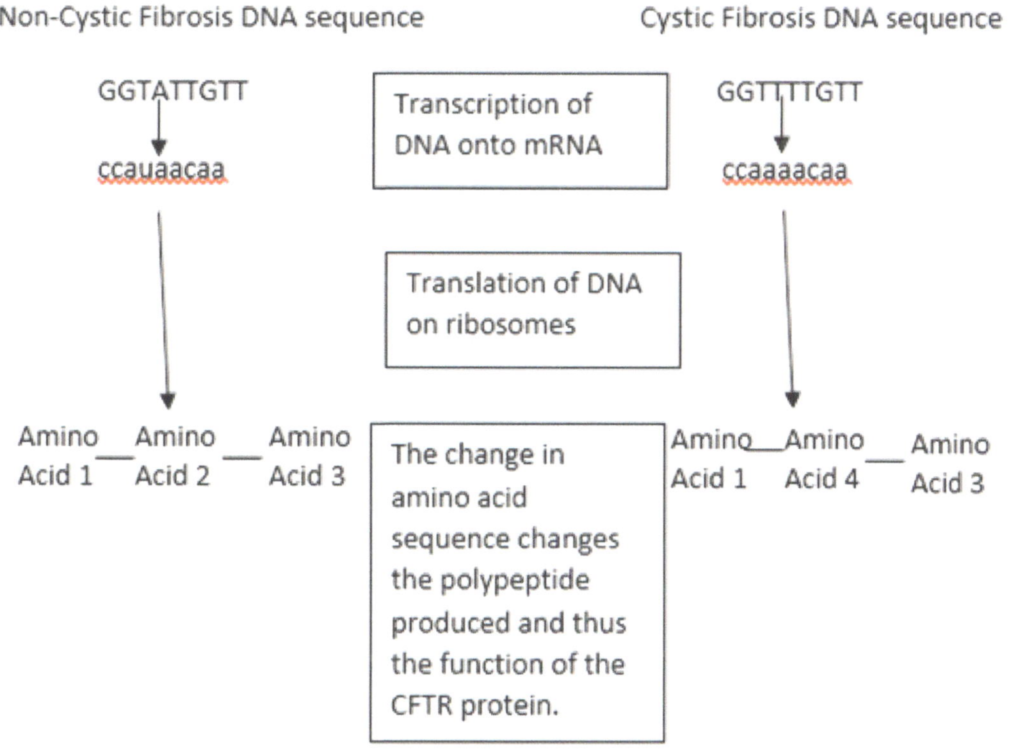

Question 23

Criteria	Marks
Description of both scientists experiments with correct conclusion stated, Direct link for each conclusion to a current method used to reduce transmission of infectious diseases.	6
Description of both scientists experiments with correct conclusion stated, Direct link for one conclusion to current method to reduce transmission and inferred for one conclusion.	4-5
Description of both scientists experiments conclusions inferred and a link to current method of reducing transmission.	3
Description of both scientists experiments with correct conclusion stated. OR Outline of both scientist work and a link to current method of reducing transmission	2
Some relevant information about scientists or a link between scientists and current method.	1

Sample answer:
Louis Pasteur performed his famous swan neck experiment where an open sterilised nutrient broth was exposed to air, while another sterilised nutrient broth was not exposed to air. The exposed broth developed microbial growth. This lead to his Germ Theory of disease, that microorganisms are present in air and exposure can lead to disease. Robert Koch, performed his experiment by developing a method to culture microorganisms. He removed samples from infected animals, grew the microorganisms in culture and then infected healthy animals. These animals became sick and the same microorganisms where found in the deliberately infected organism as the original source. He concluded that a specific disease was caused by the presence of a specific microorganisms. Today we use Pasteur's method of heating food and water to remove or reduce the number of microorganisms in these foods. This interrupts the transfer of microorganisms which may lead to infectious diseases, causing a reduction in the spread of these diseases. The use of vaccines today is a direct result of Koch work to identify the microorganism that cause specific disease. This lead to techniques such as genetic engineering to develop altered versions of these microorganisms which could be used to cause an immune response to remove the microorganisms should the host be exposed. This has reduced both number of occurrences of and transmission of these diseases.

Question 24 (a)

Criteria	Marks
Correctly annotates diagram	1

Sample answer:

Question 24 (b)

Criteria	Marks
Correctly identifies process, links to meiosis, gives detail of characteristic of process and result.	4
Correctly identifies process, links to meiosis, gives detail of characteristic of process.	3
Correctly identifies process, links to meiosis, gives a characteristic of process.	2
Correctly identifies process and links to results or process	1

Sample answer:
The process shown in the diagram is called crossing over. During meiosis sister chromatids arrange themselves in pairs. This close contact to similar DNA strands sometimes results in sections of DNA breaking from their original chromatid and reforming with the sister chromatid. This can result in an exchange of genetic material, creating genetic variation.

Question 25

Criteria	Marks
Correct components of feedback mechanism stimulus, receptor, transmission, effector, response; correct pathway direction and identification of return to homeostasis response removes stimulus.	5
Correct components of feedback mechanism stimulus, receptor, transmission, effector, response; correct pathway direction and no identification of return to homeostasis.	4
Most components of feedback mechanism stimulus, receptor, transmission, effector, response; correct pathway direction and no identification of return to homeostasis.	3
Some identification of feedback mechanism steps, correct response to stimulus	2
Some relevant information about a negative feedback mechanism	1

Sample answer:

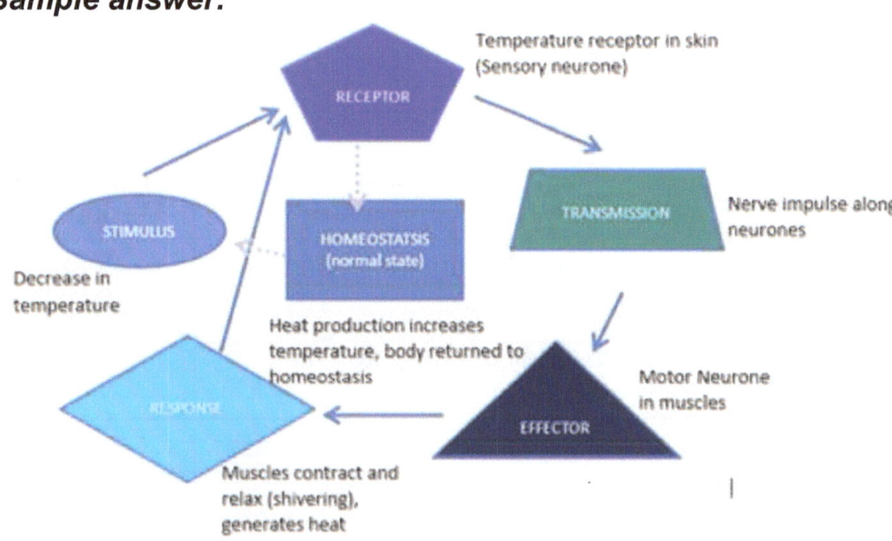

Question 26 (a)

Criteria	Marks
Correct statement including dependent and independent variable.	1

Sample answer:
Dam water will contain more microorganisms than treated water.

Question 26 (b)

Criteria	Marks
Identifies one independent variable and identified controls, including comparison plate.	3
Identifies one independent variable and use of controls	2
Identifies one independent variable OR use of controls	1

Sample answer:
The method was valid as the only variable changed was the water samples, either treated or dam water, the method to inoculate the agar plates were the controlled, same volume, same method, sterilisation of inoculation loop prior to platin, same temperature of incubation, same time. The addition of a comparison plate, an agar plate not exposed to any water sample allowed for the colonies grown to be attributed to the water samples only and as a result of contamination.

Question 26 (c)

Criteria	Marks
Describes how data collected and links to presentation choice.	4
Describes how data collected and states presentation choice	3
Outlines how data collected and states presentation choice	2
States how data collected and presented	1

Sample answer:
1mm grid transparencies were placed over the agar plates and counts of the coverage by microbial colonies were taken. This resulted in quantitative values being collected from each agar plate. The same method was followed for the control plates which allows for the subtraction of any colonies grown on these plates. This was presented in a table for each plate and averages were calculated and included in the table. The table allows for easy and clear presentation of data and comparison between the treated and dam water.

Question 27 (a)

Criteria	Marks
Type of compound identified	1

Sample answer: Protein

Question 27 (b)

Criteria	Marks
Explanation in terms of differential survival and subsequent passing on of resistance to offspring.	2
One of the above	1

Sample answer:
Some individual insects may possess a genetic variation which makes them less susceptible to the toxin. They will survive and reproduce more successfully than the others. This resistance will be passed to their offspring and will become much more widespread in the population.

Question 27 (c)

Criteria	Marks
One implication for society outlined and assessed – points for and/or against given. One implication for the environment outlined and assessed – points for and/or against given	4
One of the above assessed, the other just outlined.	3
One implication assessed OR both just outlined.	2
One implication outlined.	1

Sample answer:
Bt crops are more successful than conventional ones – on a large scale they are more economical. One positive implication for society is that this will allow more efficient large scale food production – resulting in more, cheaper food available for people. One negative implication is the fact that these crops are owned by large agribusinesses. Poor, small scale farmers will not be able to afford to grow them, they will be less competitive against the larger farmers and third world subsistence communities will be disadvantaged. One environmental implication will be the reduction in use of pesticides, this will be good for nearby natural ecosystems as these chemicals will be removed from their food chains. It will also have positive health implications for agricultural workers working with the crops.

Question 27 (d)

Criteria	Marks
One ethical argument outlined. Explanation of why some people might hold to that view	2
One of the above.	1

Sample answer:
Some religious people hold to the view that people do not have the right to interfere with species created by God. This view derives from their religious convictions. Creating Bt crops involves mixing genetic material from two species that would never normally come together.

Question 28

Criteria	Marks
Makes a judgement about the effect cell replication has in both unicellular and multicellular organisms (with examples) and links this to the continuation of a species	4
Describes the effect cell replication has in both unicellular and multicellular organisms (with examples) and links this to the continuation of a species	3
Describes the effect cell replication has in both unicellular and multicellular organisms (with examples)	2
Describes the effect or provides an example of cell replication in either unicellular or multicellular organisms.	1

Sample answer:
Cell replication is essential for the continuity of a species. It is needed in both mitosis and meiosis. In multicellular organisms exact copies of cells are needed for growth and repair of tissues and organs. Cell replication is essential for the reproduction of unicellular organisms, for example binary fission in bacteria.
In organisms which reproduce sexually. DNA needs to replicate and cells need to divide to produce daughter cells with half the number of chromosomes.
So without it, unicellular organisms couldn't reproduce and neither could multicellular organisms – so it is essential if a species is to continue to exist.

Question 29 (a)

Criteria	Marks
To sterilise the flask making sure no microorganisms are present before the experiment.	1

Question 29 (b)

Criteria	Marks
Both independent and dependent variable correctly identified	1

Sample answer:
Growth of the microorganisms
Shape of the opening of the flask

Question 29 (c)

Criteria	Marks
Repetition of experiment	1

Question 29 (d)

Criteria	Marks
Explains the reason why no growth occurred in the flask with the curve in it even though both flasks were open to the air.	2
Partly explains that microorganisms are present in the air which causes the tea to spoil.	1

Question 30 (a)

Criteria	Marks
Describes differences and one similarity	3
Describes differences	2
Identifies one difference	1

Sample answer:
DNA sequencing and profiling both use the technologies of Polymerase chain reaction and gel electrophoresis. DNA sequencing determines the order of nucleotides in a DNA molecule while DNA profiling compares DNA fragments to determine similarities or differences between individuals. DNA sequencing is a more costly and time consuming process than DNA profiling which is quick and inexpensive.

Question 30 (b)

Criteria	Marks
With reference to diagram, highlight similarities and between child and parents and criteria for conclusion.	4
With reference to diagram, highlight similarities between child and some parents and criteria for conclusion.	3
Highlights some similarities between child and parents and a conclusion	2
Some relevant link.	1

Sample answer:
The mother and child have three microsatellites in common the other microsatellites must come from the father. Father 1 and the child have 4 microsatellites in common, father 2 has 3 microsatellites in common, while father 3 has only two microsatellites in common. From this Father 1 is the most likely candidate for child's father.

Question 31

Criteria	Marks
Explains the benefits of such campaigns	3
Explains a benefits of such campaigns Or Outlines benefits of campaigns	2
Some relevant information	1

Sample answer:
As with many cancers early detection increases survival rates. By offering free screening for breast cancer, the financial burden of testing is removed from those in our society that are unlikely to seek testing, this means the detection of cancer is early, result in the treatment being less invasive, reducing costs to our hospital system and less interruption to people's lives including work and their financial balance. It also reduces suffering as less people die from breast cancer, due to early detection.

Question 32

Criteria	Marks
Identifies non-infectious, states use of survey for all possible causes, data for both sufferers and non-sufferers in preschool environment, eliminates commonality, possible further investigation.	8-9
Identifies non-infectious, states use of survey for all possible causes, data for both sufferers and non-sufferers in preschool environment, eliminates commonality.	6-7
Identifies non-infectious, states use of survey for all possible causes, data for both sufferers and non-sufferers, eliminates commonality.	4-5
Identifies non-infectious, states use of survey for both sufferers and non-sufferers, outlines cause, eliminates commonality.	3-4
States use of survey for both sufferers and non-sufferers, outlines cause, eliminates commonality. OR States use of comparison between sufferers and non-sufferers	1-2

Sample answer:

As the symptoms do not appear to be transmitted to family members this indicates the disease is a result of direct contact with the cause at the preschool. All members of the preschool would need to be surveyed to determine what activities or materials were used to during the week the symptoms appeared. Things could include, new materials for craft such as glue, new hand wash, use of disinfectants. Play areas would also need to be included in the survey and food and water or preparation areas. A comparison between those who have developed the symptoms and those that have not developed the symptoms would need to be done. By eliminating the common activities, materials etc used by all, these can be discounted as the source of the disease. Those activities or materials etc, that were used, interacted with etc those who have the symptoms would then be identified as the most likely cause. To confirm which one is the cause, all those materials etc should be removed from the preschool and further testing away from the children should occur by reintroducing them one at a time back into use.

Question 33 (a)

Criteria	Marks
Gives loss of function due to correct loss of structure, gives detailed description of how implant replaces structure and link to function.	4
Gives loss of function due to correct loss of structure, gives a description of how implant replaces structure and link to function.	3
Gives loss of function due to correct loss of structure, gives outline of how implant replaces structure and link to function.	2
Gives loss of function due to correct loss of structure, or links replaced structure to loss of structure	1

Sample answer:
The cochlear implant is used to replicate the action of the hair cells in the cochlea. These hair cells sit in the organ of corti and when stimulated these hair cells secrete a neurotransmitter which is transferred to the auditory nerve, which the brain then decodes as sound. When these hair cells are damaged or broken, no impulse is produced and thus no sound is decoded by the brain causing deafness. The cochlea implant replaces those hair cells by the thin electrode wire causing the electrical stimulation of the nerves in membrane to send an impulse to the auditory nerve which the brain decodes as sound.

Question 33 (b)

Criteria	Marks
Judgement supported by described criteria.	3
Judgement supported by outlined criteria.	2
Judgement with referred criteria.	1

Sample answer:
The cochlear implant is an extremely effective form of technology to assist in hearing loss. All other technologies, hearing aid and bone implants, still rely on the hair cells picking up the vibrations to send to the brain. The cochlear implant overcomes the loss of the sensory neurones, hair cells, that are not functioning for whatever reason. Giving the sense of hearing to those who have never been able to hear before or those who have lost their hearing entirely due to illness, accident etc.

Question 34

Criteria	Marks
Identifies a valid conservation programme, use of genetic technology and detailed description of how it is being used.	4
Identifies a valid conservation programme, use of genetic technology and an outline of how it is being used.	3
Identifies a valid conservation programme and an outline of how genetics being used.	2
Some relevant information.	1

Sample answer:
By sequencing the DNA of the koala populations is a measure being used to conserve the endangered species. This process allows for genetic diversity to be mapped and identification of immunity to diseases that affect the population. This information allows for breeding programmes to be developed where koalas who have the genetic information that creates immunity to diseases such as chlamydia can be introduced into populations where immunity is low, thus creating a new variation within the population that increases the chances of the koala's survival. Plus, the use of this information can be used to increase genetic diversity in populations by moving males or females into different populations to produce greater genetic variety in the population as the lowering of genetic diversity decreases the koalas' survival chances.

Question 35

Criteria	Marks
Correct adaptation of named pathogen and how assists invasion	2
Correct adaptation of named pathogen and reference to assisting invasion	1

Sample answer:
Bacterial cells can produce a capsule surrounding their cells which resist phagocytosis by host cells.

2020 PRELIMINARY EXAMINATION

Biology

General Instructions	• Reading time – 5 minutes • Working time – 2 hours • Write using black pen • Draw diagrams using pencil • Calculators approved by NESA may be used
Total marks: 75	Section I – 20 marks (pages 1–8) • Attempt Questions 1–20 • Allow about 35 minutes for this section
	Section II – 55 marks (pages 9–18) • Attempt Questions 21–32 • Allow about 1 hours and 25 minutes for this section

LMC Lachlan Macquarie College

Section I

20 marks
Attempt Questions 1–20
Allow about 35 minutes for this section

Use the multiple-choice answer sheet for Questions 1–20.

1. Which of the following contains only cell requirements?

   A. Lipids, Proteins, Urea
   B. Lipids, Proteins, Carbon Dioxide
   C. Lipids, Nucleic Acids, Proteins
   D. Lipids, Nucleic Acids, Urea

2. In transpiration, the function of the stomata is

   A. to bring in nutrients from the soil.
   B. gaseous exchange.
   C. to deliver water to the roots.
   D. add rigidity to the stem.

3. The data collected for the Finches of the Galapagos Islands was from

   A. Darwin's Theory of Evolution by Natural Selection
   B. Spontaneous generation
   C. Lamarck evolution
   D. Genetic Drift

4. The movement of materials like sugars in plants from the leaves to other parts of the plant is called

   A. transpiration.
   B. absorption.
   C. adhesion.
   D. translocation.

5. Modern day antibiotic resistant bacteria is an example of

   A. geographical isolation.
   B. evolution via natural selection.
   C. comparative embryology.
   D. artificial selection.

6. Photosynthesis is the process

   A. of making carbon dioxide gas and water.
   B. making oxygen gas and water.
   C. used by plants to get energy from sunlight and turn it into chemical energy.
   D. in which chemical energy is converted to carbon dioxide.

Use the following diagram to answer questions 7 to 9.

The enzyme catalase is found in liver tissue in mammals. It speeds up the removal of hydrogen peroxide from the body by converting it to water and oxygen.

A student set up the following investigation to determine if pH affects the rate at which catalase converts hydrogen peroxide to water and oxygen.

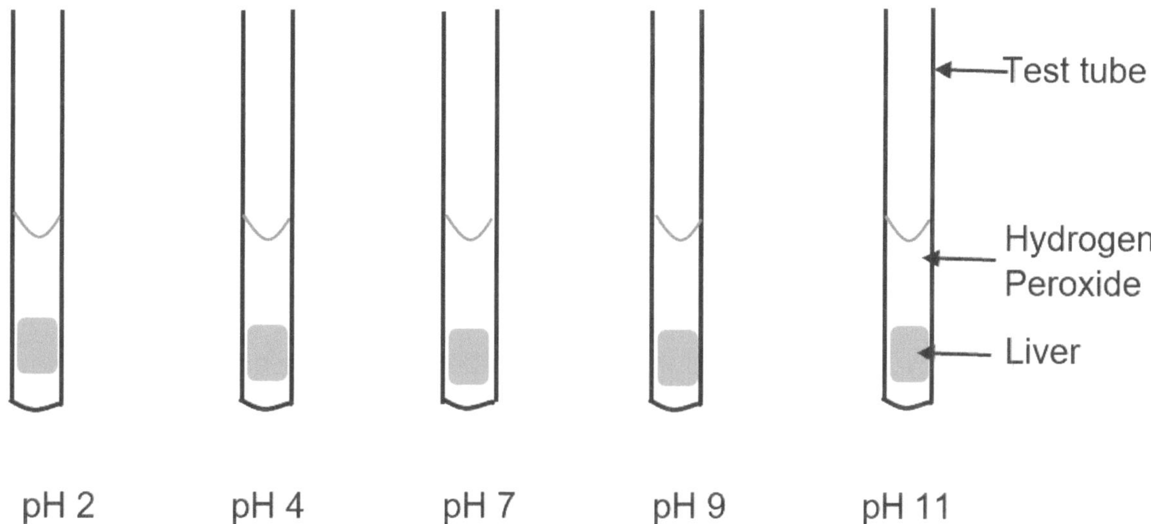

7. Which of the following would be a controlled variable in this investigation?

   A. Liver from 5 different mammals.
   B. Changing the pH.
   C. The amount of oxygen bubbles produced.
   D. The temperature at which the investigation is conducted.

8. Which of the graphs below would best represent the results?

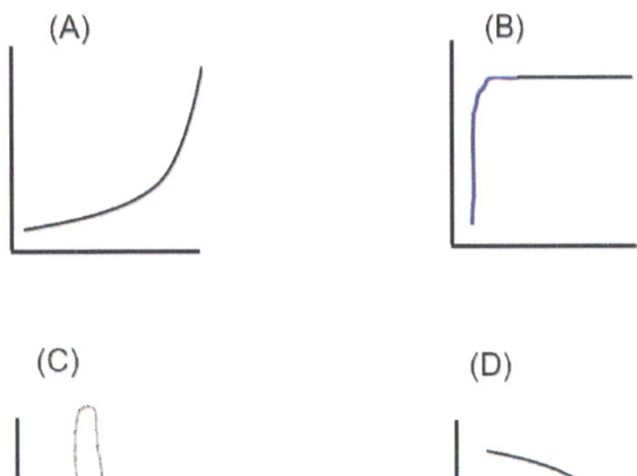

9. When an enzyme loses the active site shape, it is said to

   A. have denatured.
   B. be pH specific.
   C. be substrate specific.
   D. be temperature specific.

10. The diagram below represents two theories as to how natural selection could have occurred.

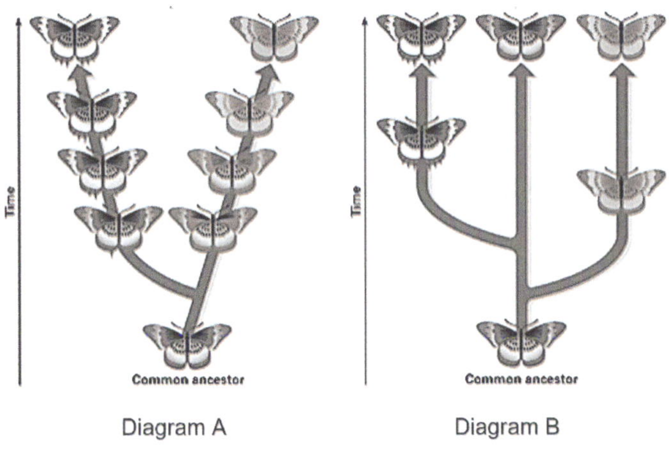

Diagram A Diagram B

https://bodell.mtchs.org/OnlineBio/BIOCD/text/chapter15/concept15.1.html accessed 19/6/10 2.00pm

Diagram B represents the model known as:

   A. Gradualism
   B. Punctuated Equilibrium
   C. Biogeography
   D. Embryology

11. On the Great Barrier Reef, clown fish can be regularly seen swimming in and around sea anemones (just like in the movie Finding Nemo). The anemone provides shelter and protection for the fish and the clown fish provides nutrients for the anemone.

    This relationship is an example of

    A. Commensalism
    B. Mutualism
    C. Parasitism
    D. Predation

12. Students in year 11 visited a marine rock platform and were asked to record how the distribution of plants varied as you moved from the low tide mark to the splash zone (further up towards the beach). The best method to do this would be using:

    A. A transect
    B. Quadrats
    C. Capture re-capture
    D. Point sampling

13. One piece of evidence which suggests Australia's ecosystem has changed is that marine animal fossils have been found in outback Australia, dating around 65–140 million years ago.

    From this evidence we can infer that:

    A. Swampy environments existed in the Sydney basin during the Permian period 298 million years ago.
    B. Australia's climate has shifted to being warmer and drier in more recent years.
    C. Australia previously had active volcanoes that erupted around this time.
    D. An inland ocean covered parts of outback Australia during these times.

14. Earthworms feed on non-living organic material including fruits, remains of dead plants and animals and also wastes that accumulate in the soil.

    This type of heterotrophic consumer would be best described as a:

    A. Scavenger
    B. Omnivore
    C. Parasite
    D. Detritus feeder

15. The hierarchical structure of an organism is

    A. systems, organs, cells, organelles and tissues.
    B. cells, organelles, tissues, systems and organs.
    C. organelles, cells, tissues, organs and systems.
    D. cells, tissues, organelles, organs and systems.

16. The difference between unicellular and multicellular organisms is

    A. Unicellular organisms are made up of only one cell while multicellular organisms are composed of more than one cell
    B. Unicellular organisms are eukaryotic while multicellular organisms are prokaryotic
    C. Unicellular organisms have membrane bound organelles while multicellular organisms do not.
    D. Unicellular organisms are always autotrophs while multicellular are heterotrophs

17. What are selection pressures in ecosystems?

    A. The abiotic features
    B. The biotic features
    C. Changes in environments due to human impacts
    D. Changes in environments that limit a resource creating competition.

18.

The above graph shows a measure of carbon dioxide levels taken from ice cores over the last 13 or so years.

From this information the best conclusion which could be made is:

A. By 2030 carbon dioxide levels will be around 450ppm
B. Carbon dioxide levels in the atmosphere have increased at a steady rate of approximately 2ppm per year each year for the last 13 years.
C. The burning of fossil fuels has increased over the last 13 years
D. More forests have been cleared to make way for houses

19.

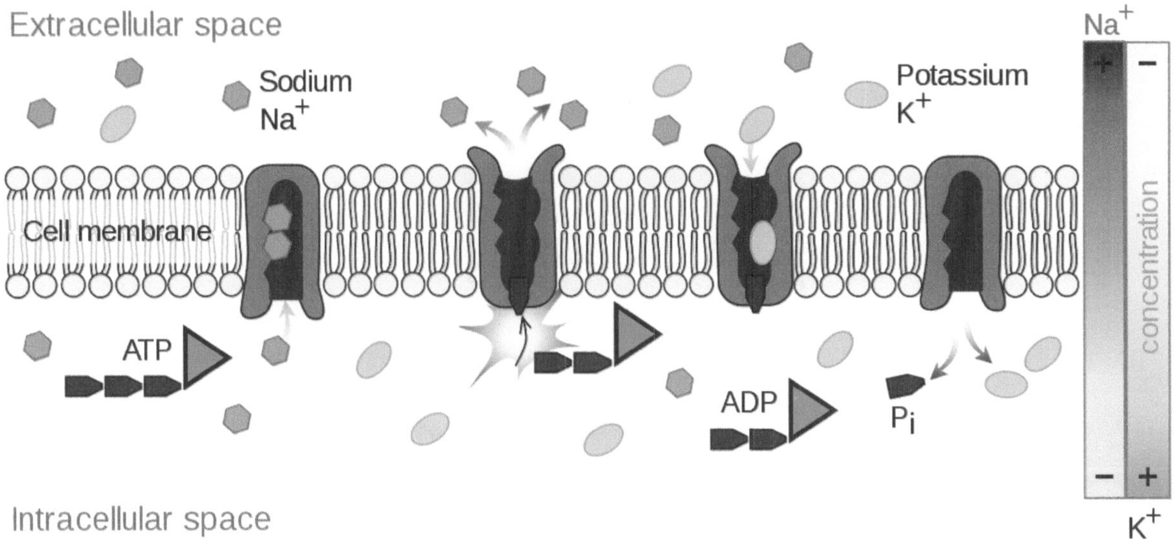

What type of transport is represented by the diagram?

A. Passive
B. Active
C. Osmosis
D. Diffusion

20. When mining activities occur throughout the world certain habitat areas can be cut off from one another leaving them isolated. This then can lead to smaller population sizes and the extinction of species.

This is mainly due to:

A. There are too many individuals in the one small area
B. Habitat is lost, gene flow is restricted and inbreeding occurs
C. Small populations are unable to breed
D. Other species will migrate out of the area.

2020 TRIAL HIGHER SCHOOL CERTIFICATE EXAMINATION	
Biology Section II Answer Booklet	Centre Number Student Number
55 marks **Attempt Questions 21–32** **Allow about 1 hours and 25 minutes for this section**	

Instructions	• Write your Centre Number and Student Number at the top of this page • Answer the questions in the spaces provided. These spaces provide guidance for the expected length of response. • Show all relevant working in questions involving calculations.

Please turn over

Question 21 (4 marks)

In the space provided, draw an annotated diagram of the fluid mosaic model of the cell membrane. 4

....
....
....
....
....
....

Question 22 (4 marks)

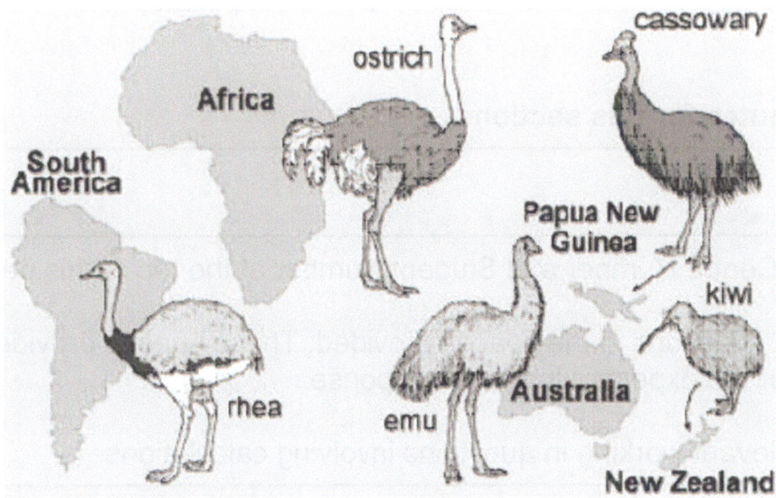

https://youngzine.org/news/our-earth/mystery-flightless-birds accessed 19/6/20 1.000pm

The diagram above shows the distribution of the modern Ratites, flightless birds. Using this information and information you gathered while studying Module 3 Biological Diversity, explain how this information could be used to support Charles Darwin's theory of evolution by natural selection. 4

....
....
....
....
....
....
....
....

Question 23 (4 marks)

Compare and contrast the mechanism of gaseous exchange between mammals and fish. 4

....
....
....
....
....
....
....

Question 24 (4 marks)

(a) Describe the method and results of an experiment you performed in class that showed the function xylem vessels. 2

....
....
....
....
....
....

(b) Draw a fully labelled method of the experimental setup. 2

Question 25 (5 marks)

(a) Label the following diagram of the digestive system. 3

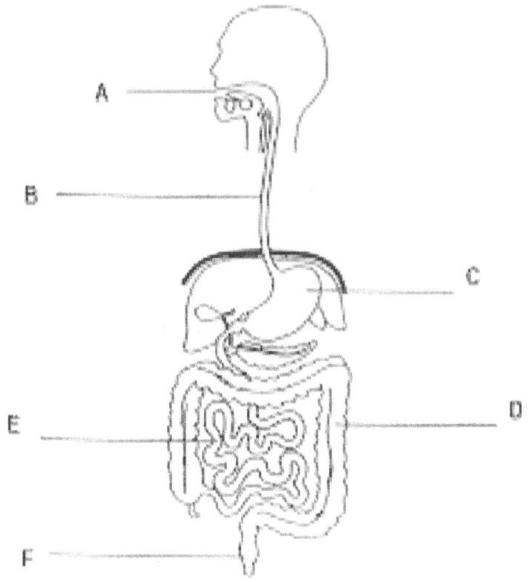

(b) Explain how food is assimilated by the body. 2

Question 26 (5 marks)

(a) The following diagrams show two organelles found in cells that are involved in energy production. 1

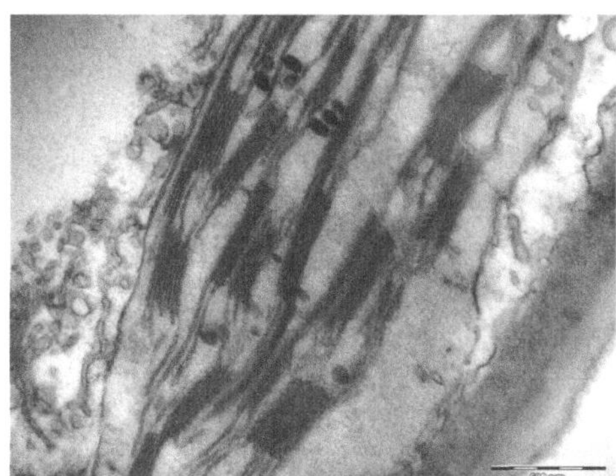

Diagram X

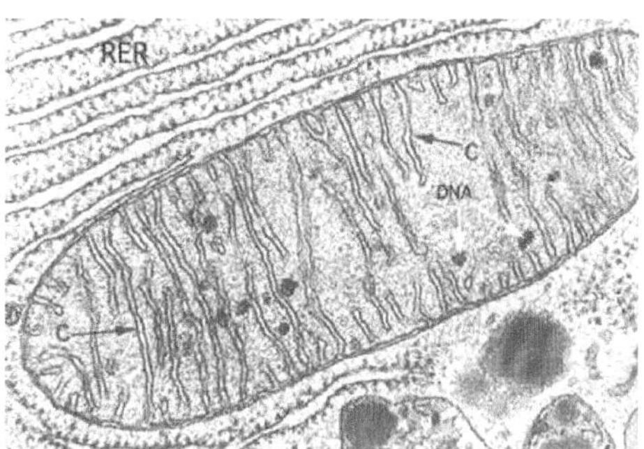

Diagram Y

Identify the organelle in Diagram X and Diagram Y.

Diagram X ....
Diagram Y ....

(b) Construct a table to compare these two organelles, include in your comparison their roles in energy production. 4

Question 27 (7 marks)

The diagram below shows rhubarb skin under the microscope under different conditions.

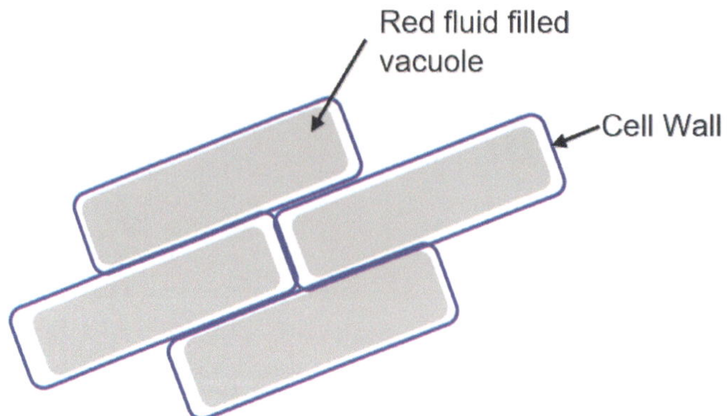

Wet Mount of Rhubarb skin
X400

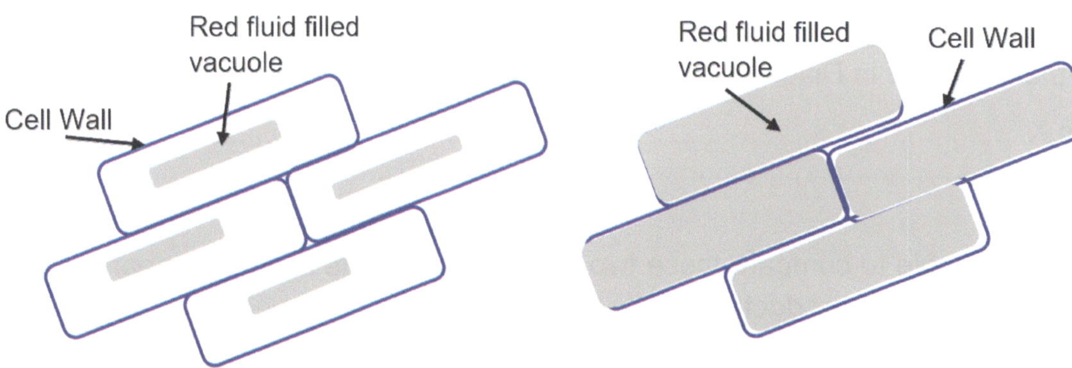

Wet Mount of Rhubarb skin
Slide flushed with salt water
X400

Wet Mount of Rhubarb skin
Slide flushed with distilled water
X400

(a) The diagrams are drawn to scale, estimate the size of the rhubarb cells. 2

....

....

(b) Identify the processes being observed. 1

....

....

....

....

(c) Explain the results obtained after the slide was flushed with salt water then flushed with distilled water. 4

....

....

....

....

Question 28 (5 marks)

(a) Define cell differentiation and explain why organisms need specialised cells. 3

....
....
....
....

(b) 2

Name the cell and state its function.

....
....

Question 29 (4 marks)

Explain the difference between abiotic and biotic factors. Give two examples of each. 4

....
....
....
....
....
....
....
....
....
....
....
....

Question 30 (2 marks)

Distinguish between convergent and divergent evolution. 2

....
....
....
....

Question 31 (6 marks)

Insects have an open circulatory system whereas mammals have a closed circulatory system. Describe each system and explain which system is more efficient and why. 6

....
....
....
....
....
....
....
....
....
....
....
....

Question 32 (7 marks)

The Australian Corroboree frog is an endangered species. Breeding programs at Taronga zoo are taking place in an effort to prevent it from becoming extinct.

Population estimates for these frogs are being carried out at regular intervals in suitable habitat areas using the capture -mark -recapture techniques.

The ratio of tagged to untagged animals can be used to estimate the size of the population as follows:

$$\text{Population Size } (N) = \frac{\text{Initial number captured } (C) \times \text{Number recaptured } (R)}{\text{Number tagged in recapture } (T)}$$

The table below provides data on corroboree frog (capture-recapture) over a number of years in Kosciuszko National park.

YEAR	2004	2005	2006	2007	2008	2009	2010
Initial Capture (C)	28	16	7	10	10	7	6
Recapture (R)	16	15	9	11	9	6	5
Tagged in Recapture (T)	3	3	1	2	2	1	1
Population size (N)	149						

(a) Complete the population size for each year and add them to the table above. 3
For example: in 2004 population size would be:

$$(N) = \frac{(C) \times (R)}{(T)}$$

$$N = \frac{28 \times 16}{3}$$

$$N = 149$$

(b) Complete a graph below which shows how the population size of the corroboree frog has changed from 2004 to 2010. 4

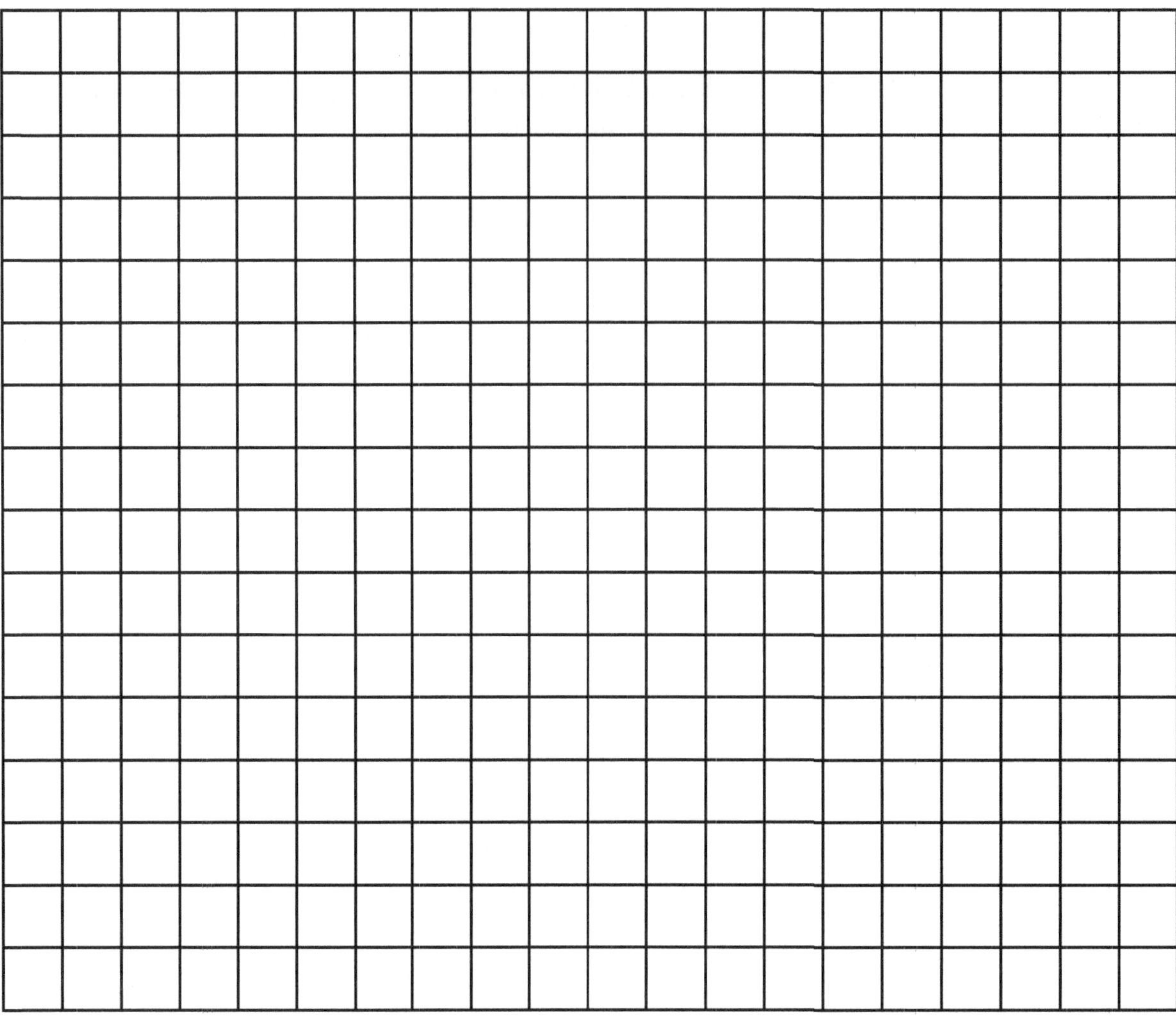

Preliminary Biology Marking Guidelines

Section I: Multiple-choice Answer Key

Question	Answer
1	C
2	B
3	A
4	D
5	B
6	C
7	D
8	C
9	A
10	B
11	B
12	D
13	D
14	D
15	C
16	A
17	D
18	D
19	B
20	B

Section II

Question 21

Criteria	Marks
• Map diagram in pencil showing bilayer and embedded protein, all detailed labels	4
• Map diagram in pencil showing bilayer and embedded protein, all simple OR some detailed labels	3
• Map diagram in pencil showing bilayer and embedded protein, some simple labels	2
• Diagram showing basic bilayer structure with a label	1

Suggested answer:
Bush medicine refers to the use of plants to treat illness, it generally is based on information gained from traditional indigenous methods of treating illnesses.

Question 22

Criteria	Mark
• Describes the information in the diagram and other information from module and relates to natural selection, describes how this supports natural selection	4
• Describes the information in the diagram and other information from module and relates to natural selection, states how this supports natural selection	3
• Outlines the information in the diagram relates to natural selection, states how this supports natural selection	2
• Some correct information linking diagram to natural selection	1

Suggested answer:
The fact that all these birds share a common characteristic, suggests they also shared a common ancestor in the past. The continents shown in the diagram, were once all joined as a larger continental mass called Gondwana. From this information it would support Darwin's idea of natural selection, as this common ancestor lived on the Gondwanan continent. As the land mass began to break up and move away from the other land masses their environments changed enough that specific characteristics were selected by those new environmental conditions for survival. For example, the modern kiwi is a small bird better adapted to the forests of New Zealand, while the Emu has long thin legs better suited to the open grasslands of Australia.

Question 23

Criteria	Marks
• Compares and contrasts the mechanism of gaseous exchange between mammals and fish in detail.	4
• Compares and contrasts the mechanism of gaseous exchange between mammals and fish	3
• outlines the mechanism of gaseous exchange in mammals and fish	2
• briefly states the mechanisms of gaseous exchange in mammals and/or fish	1

Suggested answer:
Mammals use air sacs called alveoli that are in the lungs to extract oxygen from the air whereas fish have gills that extract oxygen from water.

Question 24 (a)

Criteria	Marks
• Describe the method and results of an experiment that show the function xylem vessels	2
• Briefly states the method and results of an experiment that shows the function of xylem vessels	1

Suggested answer:
Celery experiment to show water moving in Xylem vessels of a celery stalk.

Step 1. Cut 2 celery stalks at 45 degrees. Keep the leaves on the celery.
Step 2. Place the cut end of the celery stalk in a beaker of coloured water
Step 3. Place the other celery stalk in a beaker of uncoloured water
Step 4. Observe what happens to the stalks
Step 5. After 24 hours, cut a cross-sectional piece of the celery stalks and record what you observe

Question 24 (b)

Question 25 (a)

Criteria	Marks
• Labels all 6 parts on the diagram	3
• Labels at least 4 parts on the diagram	2
• Labels at least 2 parts on the diagram	1

Suggested answer:

A-mouth
B-oesophagus
C-stomach
D-large intestine
E-small intestine
F-rectum

Question 25 (b)

Criteria	Marks
• Defines assimilation and explains how food is assimilated by the body	2
• explains that food is assimilated by the body	1

Suggested answer:
When the body assimilates food, it absorbs vitamins, minerals, and other chemicals from food. The absorption of nutrients into the body after digestion occurs via the villi in the small intestine.

Question 26 (a)

Criteria	Marks
• Correctly labels each diagram	1

Suggested answer:
Diagram X = Chloroplast
Diagram Y = Mitochondria

Question 26 (b)

Criteria	Marks
• Construction of table, role in energy production, similarity and difference	4
• Construction of table, role in energy production, similarities and/or differences	3
• Construction of table, role in energy production, similarity or difference	2
• Construction of table, role in energy production OR a similarity and a difference	1

Suggested answer:

Feature	Chloroplast	Mitochondria
Found in which cell	Eukaryotic plants	Eukaryotic Animals and plants
DNA	Contain own DNA	Contain own DNA
Role in Energy Production	Use organic material to create high energy organic molecules	Break down high energy molecules to release energy for cellular use.

Question 27 (a)

Criteria	Mark
• Correctly estimates cell size with working	2
• Correctly estimates cell size	1

Suggested answer:

Each cell measures 4 cm long, the magnification is X400

$\frac{4}{400} = 0.01$ cm or 0.1 mm or 100 μm

Question 27 (b)

Criteria	Mark
• Correctly identifies cellular process	1

Suggested answer:

osmosis

Question 27 (c)

Criteria	Mark
• Describes changes in relative concentration gradients with both salt and distilled water, defines osmosis and relates to the changes in the cells	4
• Describes changes in relative concentration gradients with salt AND/OR distilled water, defines osmosis and relates to the changes in one cell diagram	3
• Describes changes in relative concentration gradients with salt or distilled water, refers to osmosis and relates to the changes in one cell diagram	2
• Outlines changes in relative concentration gradients with salt or distilled water, refers to osmosis and relates to the changes in one cell diagram	1

Suggested answer:
When the cells were flushed with salt water, the relative concentration of water outside the cell became low, so the relative concentration of water in the cell became high. Due to osmosis (movement of water across a semi-permeable membrane, the cell membrane and wall), water moved out of the cell and the vacuole shrivels or decreases in size. When the cells were flushed with distilled water, the relative concentration of water outside the cell became high, so the relative concentration of water in the cell became low, thus water moved into the cell and the vacuole fills up or increases in size due to osmosis.

Question 28 (a)

Criteria	Marks
• Define cell differentiation and explains why organisms need specialised cells	3
• Define cell differentiation and states that cells are specialised	2
• Briefly mentions cell differentiation and specialized cells	1

Suggested answer:
Cell differentiation is when an unspecialised young cell matures to become a specialised cell. Organisms need specialised cells so that they can function independently as a tissue. These tissues form organs and systems to make a body function

Question 28 (b)

Criteria	Marks
• Name the red blood cell and states its function	2
• Names the red blood cell	1

Suggested answer:
Red Blood Cell (erythrocytes) carry oxygen around the body

Question 29

Criteria	Marks
• Explain the difference between abiotic and biotic factors. Give two examples of each.	4
• Explain the difference between abiotic and biotic factors. Give one example of each.	3
• Explain the difference between abiotic and biotic factors.	2
• Defines abiotic or biotic factors.	1

Suggested answer:
Abiotic factors are parts of an environment that are non-living. Examples of abiotic factors are sunlight, temperature, wind, water, soil.
Biotic factors are parts of an environment that are living. Examples of biotic factors are plants, animals and microorganisms

Question 30

Criteria	Marks
• Distinguishes between convergent and divergent evolution.	2
• Defines convergent and divergent evolution	1

Suggested answer:
Divergent evolution occurs when organisms show similar characteristics from a common ancestor but they are changed to better suit their individual environments. Convergent evolution is where organisms that have no common ancestor but show similar characteristics as they inhabit similar environments.

Question 31

Criteria	Marks
• Describe the insect and mammalian circulatory system and explains which system is more efficient and why.	6
• Outlines that the insect and mammalian circulatory system are different and outlines which system is more efficient and why.	5
• States that the insect and mammalian circulatory system are different and states which system is more efficient and why.	4
• Briefly states the relationship between the insect and mammalian circulatory system and mentions which is more efficient and why	3
• Briefly describes the relationship between the insect and mammalian circulatory system	2
• Briefly states mentions the insect and mammalian circulatory system	1

Suggested answer:
In an open circulatory system, the tissue fluid and blood are similar. The fluid does not spend all the time in the blood vessels and does not go directly to the cells.
Whereas, in a closed circulatory system, the blood remains in the blood vessels and is sent directly to the cells where its components are used.
Therefore, the closed circulatory system is the more efficient system

Question 32 (a)

Criteria	Marks
• All years correct	3
• At least 4 years correct	2
• At least 2 years correct	1

Suggested answer:
2005 - 80, 2006 - 63, 2007 - 55, 2008 - 45, 2009 - 42, 2010 - 30

Question 32 (b)

Criteria	Marks
• Column graph with Year (labelled) across the x-axis and population size (labelled) on the vertical axis. Correct scale on vertical axis and data from their table plotted correctly.	4
• Take a mark off for missing labels, scale or axis around the wrong way	1-3

Suggested answer:

Column graph with Year (labelled) across the x-axis and population size (labelled) on the vertical axis. Correct scale on vertical axis and data from their table plotted correctly.

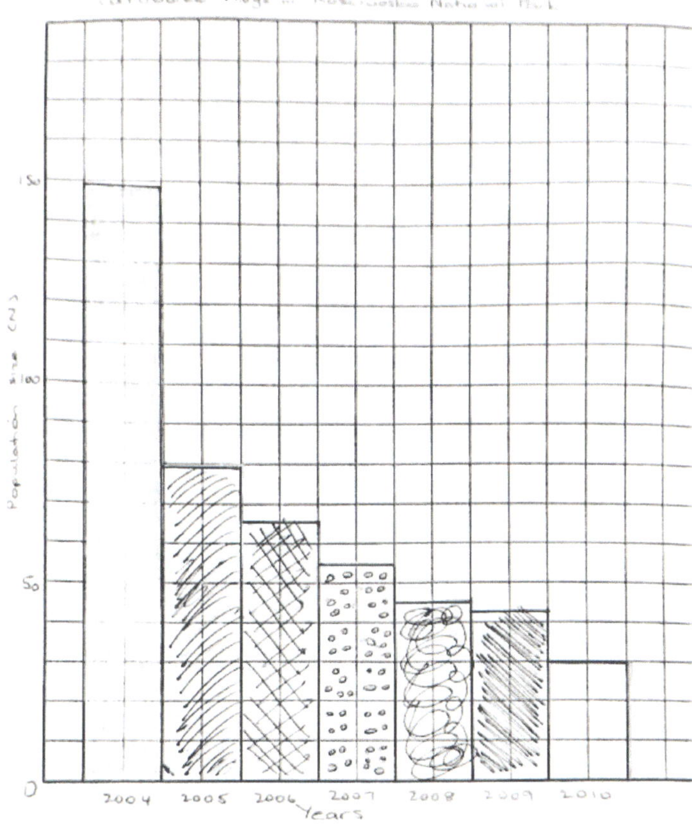

Mapping Grid

Section I

Q	Marks	Content	Syllabus Outcomes
1	1	Cell function	(1.2.2)
2	1	Nutrient and Gas requirements	(2.2.3)
3	1	Adaptations	(3.2.2)
4	1	Transport	(2.3.3)
5	1	The theory of Evolution	(3.3.2)
6	1	Nutrient and Gas requirement	(2.2.4)
7	1	Cell function	(1.2.5)
8	1	Cell function	(1.2.5)
9	1	Cell function	(1.2.5)
10	1	The theory of Evolution	(3.3.3)
11	1	Population dynamics	(4.1.2)
12	1	Population dynamics	(4.1.3)
13	1	Past ecosystems	(4.2.4)
14	1	Future ecosystems	(4.1.3)
15	1	Organisation of cells	(2.1.3)
16	1	Organisation of cells	(2.1.1)
17	1	Effects of the environment on organisms	(3.1.1)
18	1	Past ecosystems	(4.2.1)
19	1	Cell function	(1.2.1)
20	1	Future ecosystems	(4.3.4)

Section II

Q	Marks	Content	Syllabus Outcomes
21	4	Cell structure	(1.1.2)
22	4	Adaptations	(3.2.2)
23	4	Nutrient and Gas requirements	(2,2,3)
24	6	Transport	(2.3.2)
25	5	Nutrient and Gas requirements	(2.2.5)
26	3	Cell structure	(1.1.2)
27	8	Cell function	(1.2.1) WS11-4
28	5	Organisation of cells	(2.1.2)
29	6	Effects of the environment on organisms	(3.1.1)
30	2	The theory of evolution	(3.3.3)
31	6	Transport	(2.3.1)
32	7	Population dynamics	(4.1.1)

2020 TRIAL HIGHER SCHOOL CERTIFICATE EXAMINATION	
Biology	
General Instructions	• Reading time – 5 minutes • Working time – 3 hours • Write using black pen • Draw diagrams using pencil • Calculators approved by NESA may be used
Total marks: 100	Section I – 20 marks (pages 1–8) • Attempt Questions 1–20 • Allow about 35 minutes for this section
	Section II – 80 marks (pages 10–24) • Attempt Questions 21–35 • Allow about 2 hours and 25 minutes for this section
LMC Lachlan Macquarie College	

Section I

20 marks
Attempt Questions 1–20
Allow about 35 minutes for this section

Use the multiple-choice answer sheet for Questions 1–20.

1. Homeostasis is best described as:

   A. The ability to maintain a constant internal environment in response to environmental changes.
   B. The ability to change the internal environment in response to environmental changes
   C. The ability to change the internal environment to maintain water balance
   D. The ability to maintain a constant internal environment to maintain water balance

2. Two advantages of internal fertilisation are:

   A. large numbers of gametes are produced and it can only occur in water
   B. fewer gametes are produced and this results in greater variation in offspring
   C. larger numbers of gametes are produced and more offspring survive
   D. gametes are protected from dehydration and fertilised eggs are protected from predators

3.

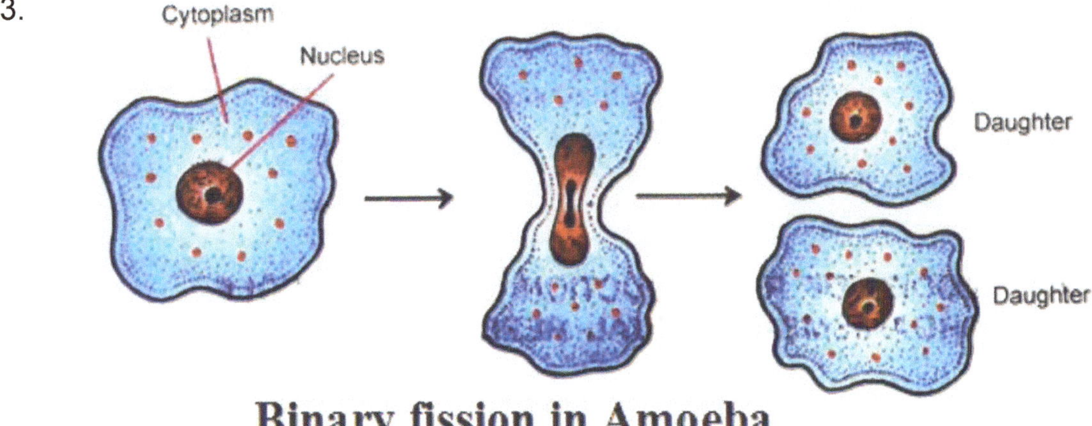

Binary fission in Amoeba

The above diagram shows a type of reproduction in Amoeba

This is:

   A. the main method of reproduction in prokaryotes and protists
   B. a type of cell division which occurs in multicellular eukaryotic organisms
   C. a form of reproduction which increases the variation in the offspring produced
   D. a way in which some bacteria can reproduce sexually

4. The amino acid sequence below is formed with the following anticodons on four transfer RNA molecules as follows:

   Amino Acid: Methionine - Arginine - Arginine - Stop
   Anticodons: UAC - UCU - UCC - ACU

   The sequence of bases on the original DNA template strand would be:

   A. AUG - AGA - AGG - UGA
   B. ATG - AGA - AGG - TGA
   C. TAC - TCT - TCC - ACT
   D. TCT - TAC - AGG - TCT

5. Radiation causes genetic mutation in somatic cells resulting in

   A. DNA being damaged resulting in an altered code in germ cells
   B. genes being passed on to the next generation
   C. tumours
   D. the death of the cell

Use diagram and information below to answer questions 6 and 7

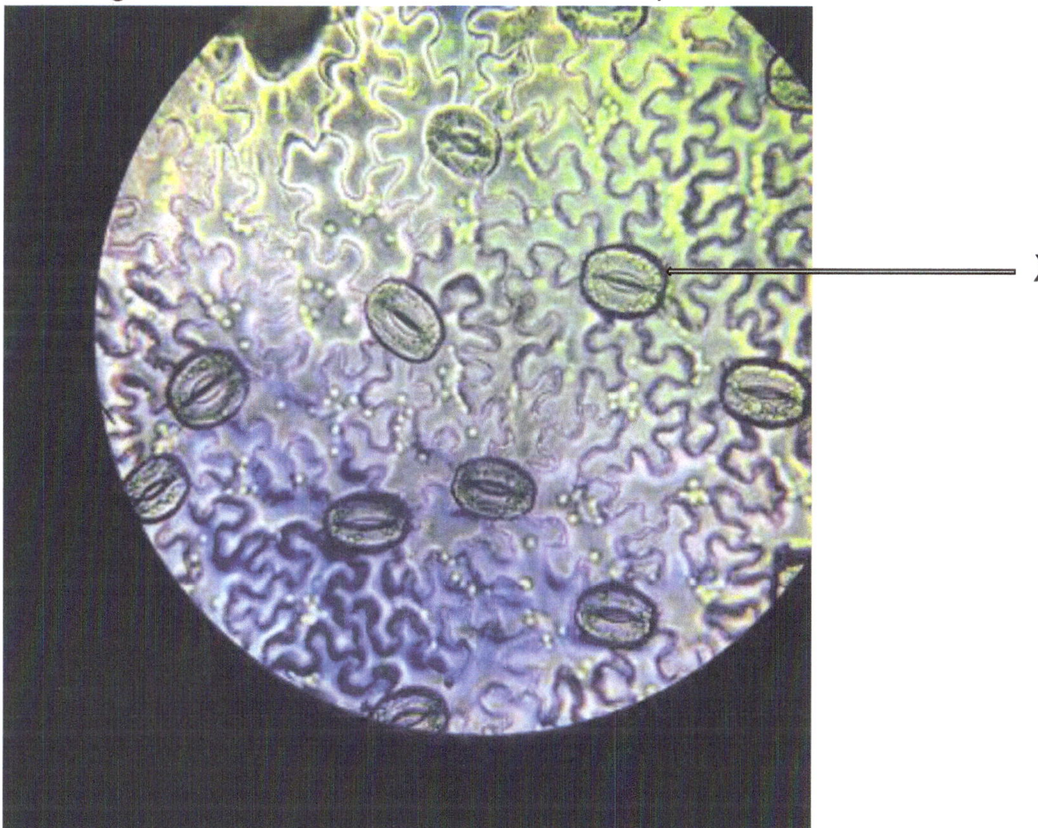

Students were investigating mechanisms in plants to conserve water. They observed the following image using a light microscope at 400X magnification.

6. Identify the structure labelled X
   A. Lenticel
   B. Root Hairs
   C. Waxy cuticle
   D. Stomate

7. Estimate the size of these structures as viewed in the diagram
   A. 1 cm
   B. 0.25 mm
   C. 2.5 μm
   D. 25 μm

8. Benefits of biotechnology on agriculture include
   A. livestock that is not adapted to its environment
   B. disease and drought resistant plants
   C. antibacterial resistance
   D. genetically modified food (GMF) that causes allergic reactions

9. A new species of plant has been discovered which seems to have 2 flower colour varieties, RED and GREEN.

   When RED varieties are crossed with RED all the offspring have RED flowers.

   When GREEN varieties are crossed with GREEN all the offspring have GREEN flowers.

   The flower inheritance pattern appears to be incomplete dominance because when a GREEN flower variety is crossed with a RED one all the offspring are BROWN

   The expected phenotypic ratios of the offspring produced when a BROWN variety is crossed with a RED are:

   A. RED : BROWN : GREEN
      1 : 2 : 1
   B. RED : BROWN
      1 : 1
   C. GREEN : BROWN
      1 : 1
   D. RED : GREEN
      1 : 1

10. Genetically engineered Human insulin is an example of
    A. recombinant DNA technology.
    B. mutation caused by a mutagen
    C. frameshift mutation
    D. Non-coding DNA segment

11. Artificial pollination results in the development of

A. small genetic pools
B. reduced chance of pollination
C. smaller yield of product
D. new varieties of plants

12. Below is a count a student made on the population of rabbits in his backyard. The wild fur colour (B) is dominant over the white fur colour (b).

Number of Rabbits	Phenotype	Genotype
20		BB
5		bb
25		Bb

The allele frequency for white fur in this population of rabbits is

A. .33
B. .05
C. .50
D. .25

13. The DNA of the fruit fly, *Drosophila melanogaster*, is arranged on five chromosomes. There are about 250 million base pairs in this DNA. From a gene pool in a population of 1,000 fruit flies living in a jar, a sample of five flies were chosen and they were allowed to breed and reproduce to the point where the population is once again 1000 flies. If the DNA of this sample possess a total of only four alleles instead of 20 different alleles like the original population,

Scientists say the number in the gene pool for the new population of fruit flies has

A. increased
B. decreased
C. remained the same
D. has doubled in number

14. Current understanding about how the virus that causes coronavirus disease 2019 (COVID-19) spreads is largely based on what is known about similar coronaviruses.

Person-to-person spread

The virus is thought to spread mainly from person-to-person.

- Between people who are in close contact with one another (within about 6 feet)
- Via respiratory droplets produced when an infected person coughs or sneezes.
- These droplets can land in the mouths or noses of people who are nearby or possibly be inhaled into the lungs.

The mode of transmission of this virus from person to person is best described as

A. direct contact
B. Indirect contact
C. Vector Transmission
D. Water borne

15. Helper T cells;

A. Produce antibodies
B. Engulf and destroy pathogens
C. Prevent the entry of pathogens into the body
D. Release chemicals which activate B cells

16. Using the mRNA sequence, which sequence shows a frameshift?

AGG GCA ACG UAC GCA C

A. A GGG CAA CGU ACG CAC
B. A GGG GCA ACG UAC GCA G
C. GGG CAA CGU ACG CAC
D. UCC CGU UGC AUG CGU G

17. Scientists are now discovering that many bioactive compounds are contained in traditional Aboriginal bush medicines. Smokebush and Tea tree leaves are just two examples of plants which contain antimicrobial properties.

    These medicines would be mainly used to treat

    A. Infectious diseases
    B. Nutritional diseases
    C. Types of Cancers
    D. Hereditary Diseases

18. The slip, slop, slap, seek and slide is a very well known preventative measure for the disease of melanoma. This form of preventative measure would be best described as

    A. Vaccination
    B. Genetic engineering
    C. Public Health campaign
    D. Hygiene practices

19. Silicosis is a group of lung diseases linked to breathing in silica dust. Which of the below would be the best group to classify this disease.

    A. Infectious
    B. Environmental
    C. Genetic
    D. Viral

20. Below is a table from the World Cancer Research Fund showing some cancer statistics in 2018.

Skin Cancer (Melanoma) Rates in Men			Skin Cancer (Melanoma) Rates in Women		
Rank	Country	Age-standardised rate per 100,000	Rank	Country	Age-standardised rate per 100,000
1	Australia	40.4	1	Denmark	33.1
2	New Zealand	35.8	2	New Zealand	31.1
3	Norway	29.0	3	Norway	30.7
4	Netherlands	26.4	4	Australia	27.5
5	Sweden	23.5	5	Sweden	26.2
6	Switzerland	23.4	6	Netherlands	25.4
7	Denmark	22.4	7	Germany	24.0
8	Germany	19.6	8	Belgium	23.9
9	Luxembourg	18.1	9	Slovenia	19.7
10	Slovenia	18.0	10	Switzerland	19.5
11=	Belgium	16.2	11	Ireland	19.0
11=	Finland	16.2	12	Finland	15.9
13=	Austria	15.0	13	Luxembourg	15.4
13=	UK	15.0	14	UK	15.3
15	US	14.9	15	France (metropolitan)	12.9
16	France (metropolitan)	14.4	16	Austria	12.6
17	Italy	14.0	17	Czech Republic	12.4
18	Ireland	13.6	18=	Canada	11.7
19	Canada	13.4	18=	Iceland	11.7
20	Czech Republic	13.3	20	Estonia	11.4

From the information provided in the above tables, you could conclude that

A. the incidence of melanoma is higher in males than females
B. overall, Australia has the highest incidence of melanoma in the world
C. the hotter the climate in the country the higher the rate of melanoma
D. women in Denmark sunbake more than men

2020 TRIAL HIGHER SCHOOL CERTIFICATE EXAMINATION	
Biology Section II Answer Booklet	Centre Number
	Student Number

80 marks
Attempt Questions 21–35
Allow about 2 hours and 25 minutes for this section

Instructions	• Write your Centre Number and Student Number at the top of this page • Answer the questions in the spaces provided. These spaces provide guidance for the expected length of response. • Show all relevant working in questions involving calculations.

Please turn over

Question 21. (3 marks)

(a) Outline the process of DNA replication 3

....
....
....
....
....
....

Question 22. (4 marks)

Below is a graph showing the relative concentrations of antibody levels in the blood showing the primary and secondary immune response.

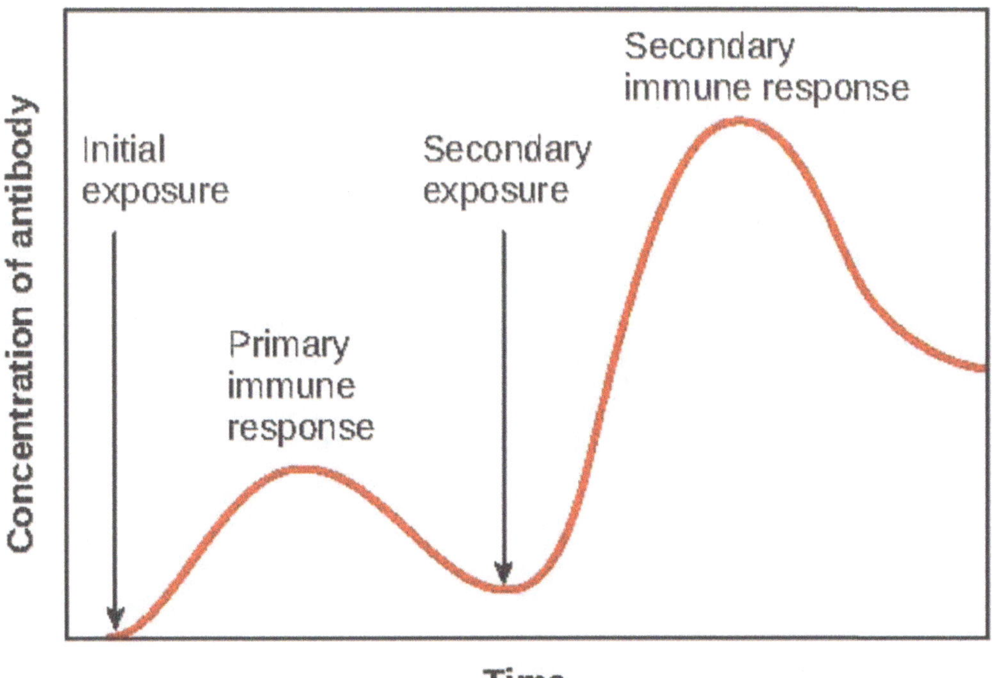

From your knowledge of Humoral immunity explain the shape of the graph. 4

....
....
....
....
....
....
....
....

Question 23. (6 marks)

When a zygote is formed from a gamete that has experienced non-disjunction, the resulting offspring will have extra or missing chromosomes in every cell of their body.

(a) Fill in the cells below showing non-disjunction occurring during meiosis 1 of the sex chromosomes. The Parent cell has XX. 3

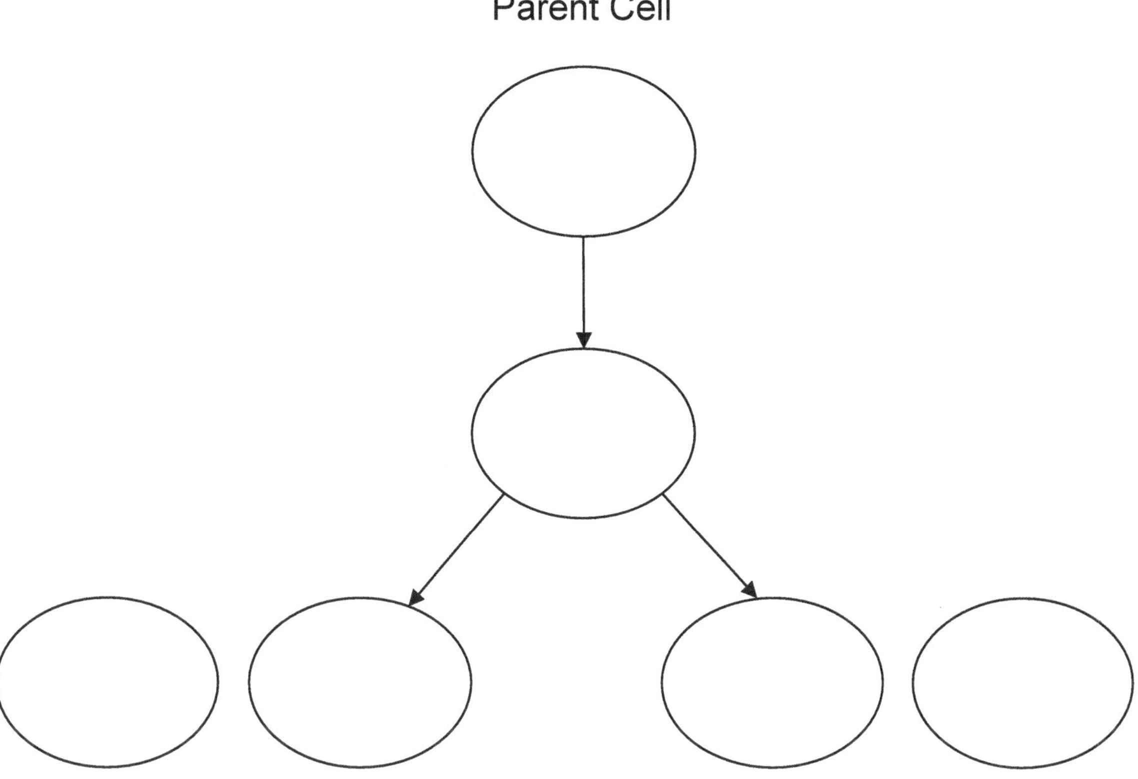

(b) Name a disorder that is caused by nondisjunction, you have studied and explain on which chromosome it is located. 3

....

....

....

....

....

....

Question 24. (8 marks)

The diagram below shows a biomedical device.

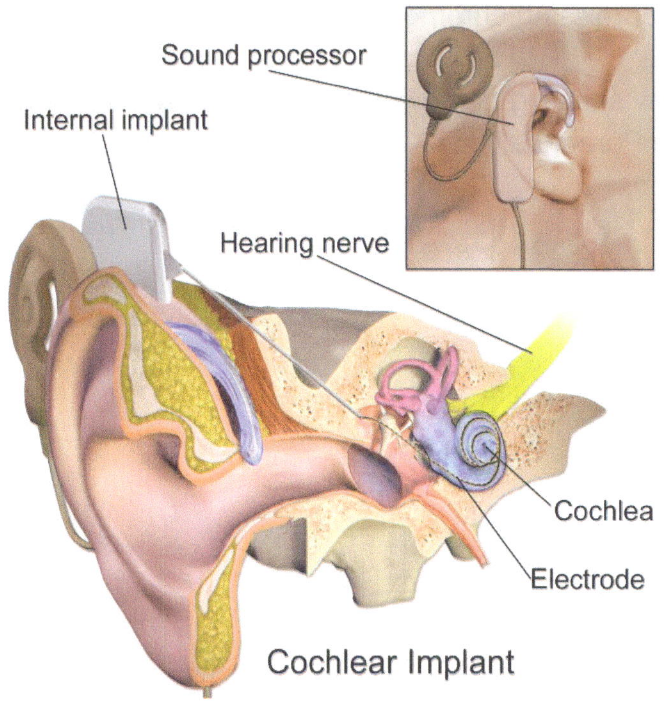

(a) Describe how the cochlear implant assists with hearing loss in relation to the structure and function of the ear. 4

....
....
....
....
....
....
....
....

(b) Assess the effectiveness of the cochlear implant to assist in the disorder of hearing loss. 4

....
....
....
....
....
....
....
....

Question 25. (6 mark)

What are the benefits of using genetic technology in society? 6

....
....
....
....
....
....
....
....
....
....
....
....
....
....
....
....

Question 26. (3 marks)

Explain how the following hygiene practices help prevent the spread of infectious diseases. 3

Washing hands, covering your mouth when coughing and tying your hair back when preparing food

....
....
....
....
....
....

Question 27. (3 marks)

The data below shows a relationship between maternal age and chromosomal errors in live births.

Maternal Age (years)	***Incidence of chromosomal error /100 live births***
<25	*0.5*
25-29	*0.6*
30-34	*1*
35-39	*1.8*
>40	*6*

(a) What is the trend shown in this table? 1

....
....

(b) Suggest a reason for this relationship. 2

....
....
....
....

Question 28. (5 marks)

Complete the table below using an infectious disease you have studied in your course 5

Name of Disease	
Cause	
Effects on Host	
Treatment /Prevention	
How the pathogen enters the body	

Question 29. (7 marks)

Dolly the sheep was cloned from a somatic cell.

(a) Explain the steps involved in this technique. 5

....
....
....
....
....
....
....
....
....
....

(b) Explain a benefit to society for this specific technique. 2

....
....
....
....

Question 30. (3 marks)

In the space below draw a negative feedback mechanism used to maintain stable blood glucose levels in humans. 3

Question 31. (5 marks)

Describe the process involved in producing a named transgenic agricultural organism using recombinant DNA technology. 6

Question 32. (8 marks)

Analyse the main phases of fertilisation in mammals and explain the importance of these phases to the continuity of a species 8

Question 33. (6 marks)

Distinguish between the terms vaccination and immunisation. In your answer explain how the two terms are related. 6

Question 34. (7 marks)

Refer to the graph below.

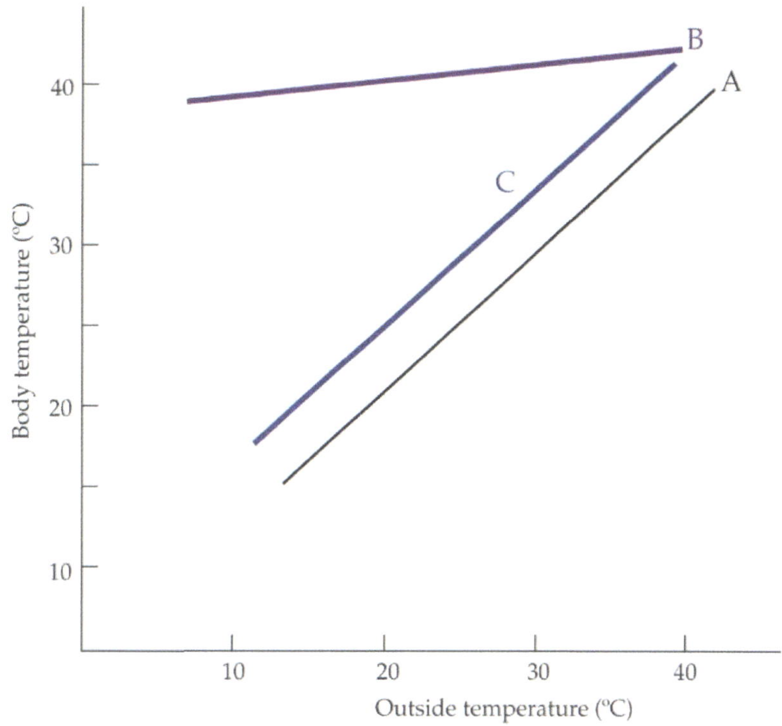

(a) Which of the lines are likely to be an ectotherm and which is likely to be an endotherm? Justify your choice. 3

....
....
....
....
....
....

(b) Describe one adaptation of both an endotherm and an ectotherm to assist in thermoregulation. 4

....
....
....
....
....
....
....
....

Question 35. (5 marks)

(a) Describe the structure and function of proteins in living things. 5

....
....
....
....
....
....
....
....
....
....

Marking Guidelines

Section I: Multiple-choice Answer Key

Question	Answer
1	A
2	D
3	A
4	C
5	C
6	D
7	D
8	B
9	B
10	A
11	D
12	D
13	B
14	B
15	D
16	B
17	A
18	C
19	B
20	B

Section II

Question 21

Criteria	Mark
• Unbinding of DNA AND complimentary binding of new nucleotides AND new strand from original strand	3
• Unbinding of DNA AND/OR complimentary binding of new nucleotides AND/OR new strand from original strand	2
• Unbinding of DNA AND/OR complimentary binding of new nucleotides	1

Suggested answer:

Double stranded DNA unzips,
Free nucleotides in cytoplasm bind to the complementary bases on each open strand,
New complementary strand formed against original strand

Question 22

Criteria	Marks
• Explains the role of B lymphocytes, plasma cells and antibodies in the immune response and links this to the shape of the graph(why the levels rise and fall)	4
• Describes the role of B-lymphocytes, plasma cells and antibodies and indicates that antibody levels change	3
• Provides some knowledge as to why antibody levels change	2
• Outlines some information about either B-cells or plasma cells or antibody function /production	1

Suggested answer:

The adaptive immune response involves the action of B & T lymphocytes.
When the body is exposed to a pathogen with antigens on its surface, a B lymphocyte with a specific antibody on its surface recognises the antigen, and binds to it. Some B cells differentiate into B memory cells while others differentiate into antibody producing plasma cells. Plasma cells secrete antibodies specific for the particular antigen. They inactivate the pathogen and mark it for destruction by phagocytes. It takes a few days for the antibody level in the blood to rise and when the pathogen is destroyed the levels lower and B-memory cells remain in the blood so if a person is reinfected with the pathogen antibody production is much faster and the pathogen is destroyed before symptoms develop.

Question 23 (a)

Criteria	Marks
• Diagram clearly shows the process of nondisjunction	3
• Some aspects were correct	2
• At least one cell filled in correctly	1

Suggested answer

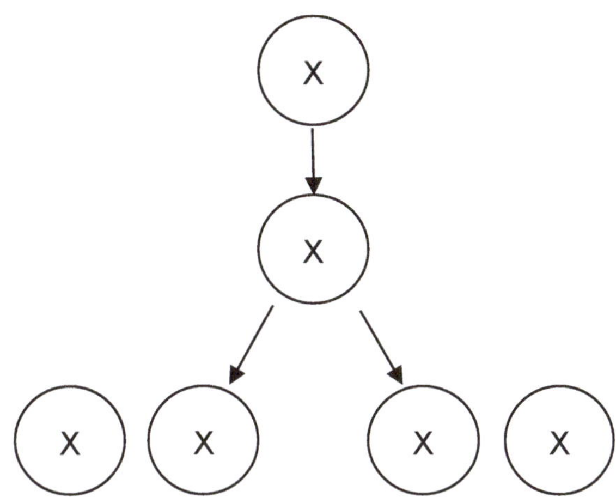

Question 23 (b)

Criteria	Marks
• Names a disorder • Correct explanation	3
• Names a disorder with a brief outline	2
• Names a disorder OR • Correct explanation	1

Suggested answer:

Downs syndrome occurs when a replication error occurs on chromosome 21 resulting in part or a whole third copy of the chromosome.

Inherited disorders: Patau's Syndrome (trisomy 13), Edwards Syndrome (trisomy 18), Down Syndrome (trisomy 21), Klinefelter Syndrome (XXY), Turner's Syndrome / Fragile X (monosomy X)

Question 24 (a)

Criteria	Marks
• Correctly describes structure and function of ear, describes how technology replicates the loss of structure and function	4
• Correctly states structure and function of ear, outlines how technology replicates the loss of structure and function	3
• Correctly states structure and function of ear, links technology to loss of function	2
• Correctly states structure and function of ear OR identifies replacement technology of structure	1

Suggested answer:
The cochlear implant is designed to replace the loss or damage of the receptor hair cells along the basal membrane in the cochlear. These hair cells detect the vibrations of sound and their movement stimulates the nerve impulse which is sent via the auditory nerve to the brain so the sound can be "heard". The cochlear implant uses a fine wire designed to cause the stimulation of the basal membrane it detects vibrations, and creates the impulse that is sent to the brain via the auditory nerve, thus replacing the action of the hair cell.

Question 24 (b)

Criteria	Mark
• Makes a valid judgement of effectiveness and describes the criteria for judgement, improvement of technology outlined	4
• Makes a valid judgement of effectiveness and describes the criteria for judgement.	3
• Makes a valid judgement of effectiveness and outlines the criteria for judgement	2
• Makes a valid judgement of effectiveness and links to improvement in disorder	1

Suggested answer:
The cochlear implant is an extremely effective form of technology used to manage and assist in hearing loss. Patients with a cochlear implant have profound hearing loss and have no sound recognition at all, thus the cochlear implant reinstates this sound recognition, so it is extremely effective in assisting manage the effects of hearing loss. The sound range produced is very limited and significantly distorted compared to that of a person with no hearing loss, but this will continue to improve as the technology itself improves, but the overall effect is restoration of hearing in those people with no hearing.

Question 25

Criteria	Marks
• Shows a thorough understanding of genetic technology • Clearly relates the use of genetic technology to benefits for society with multiple examples	5–6
• Shows a sound understanding of genetic technology • Clearly relates the use of genetic technology to benefits for society with an example	3– 4
• Shows a sound understanding of genetic technology	2
• Shows some understanding of genetic technology	1

Suggested answer:

Agricultural benefits — transgenic technologies can produce crop and animal varieties that are better suited to specific environments. Increased productivity and increased nutrient levels in animals and plants. For example, GM Atlantic Salmon which is larger and faster growing than non-GM salmon

Medical benefits — The study of cells and DNA have the potential to influence oncology, pharmaceutical and identification of non-inherited diseases in individuals. For example, recombinant DNA technology in the production of insulin

Industrial Benefits — potential GM plants that can replace non-recyclable products. Enzyme production that can be used in the food industry that is pure and can be produced efficiently and in an affordable manner

Question 26

Criteria	Marks
• Explains how each of the 3 hygiene practices prevents the spread of disease	3
• Describes how at least 2 of the 3 hygiene practices prevents disease	2
• Outlines how any one of the practices may prevent the spread of disease	1

Suggested answer:
Many types of infectious diseases are caused by microorganisms, bacteria and viruses.

They often invade a human by being ingested or inhaled and this leads to disease.

Washing hands before eating or greeting people removes possible pathogens from your skin so they are not transferred to other people or food. This helps prevent potential pathogens from being ingested.

Many diseases eg: influenza, can be spread from people inhaling viral particles in the air from an infected person. Covering your mouth while coughing reduces the chances of pathogens being spread to individuals nearby.

When preparing food it is important hygiene practices are followed. Hair may contain bacteria and if added to food may cause disease. Tying long hair back prevents hair from falling in food

Question 27 (a)

Criteria	Marks
• Correctly identifies the trend	1

Suggested answer:
There is a strong correlation between maternal age and the occurrence of non-disjunction.

Question 27 (b)

Criteria	Marks
• Correctly identifies a reason with some elaboration	2
• Correctly identifies a reason	1

Suggested answer:
This may be due to oogenesis where the developing oocytes are arrested in prophase I until ovulation.

Question 28

Criteria	Marks
Names an infectious disease, identifies the specific pathogen responsible, lists 2 effects on the host, names a treatment or preventative measure and describes how the pathogen enters the body	5
Names an infectious disease and identifies the type of pathogen and has at least 2 of – EFFECTS or TREATMENT or HOW IT ENTERS the body	4
Names an infectious disease and has at least 2 of – EFFECTS or TREATMENT or HOW IT ENTERS the body	3
Names an infectious disease and lists an effect on the host OR treatment. OR Names a non-infectious disease with an effect on the person	2
Names an infectious disease	1

Suggested answer:

Name of Disease	Tetanus
Cause	Bacteria, Clostridium tetani
Effect on Host	Bacteria makes a toxin in the body which causes muscle spasms, fits, an inability to open your mouth, which can lead to suffocation, high blood pressure and heart attack
Treatment / Prevention	The bacteria live in the soil and enter the body through cuts. Vaccinations are available and booster injections need to be given every 10 years to prevent infection.
How the pathogen enters the body	The bacteria live in the soil and enter the body through cuts.

Question 29 (a)

Criteria	Marks
• Exhibits a clear and logical sequence • Each step is clearly explained • Appropriate scientific language is used.	5
• Each step is clearly explained • Appropriate scientific language is used.	4
• Each step is clearly outlined • Appropriate scientific language is used	3
• Each step is clearly outlined	2
• some relevant information	1

Suggested answer:

- somatic cells from the udder of a sheep number 1 is removed
- nucleus of a healthy unfertilised ovum was removed from sheep number 2
- the udder cell with a nucleus from sheep 1was injected into the enucleated egg of sheep 2 and treated with electricity which caused them to fuse
- The fertilised egg multiplied and formed an embryo
- Embryo was implanted in sheep number 3
- Embryo developed into a clone of sheep number 1

Question 29 (b)

Criteria	Marks
• A relevant benefit is explained	2
• Some relevant information	1

Organ replacement — cloning allows scientists to take small amounts of cells from a certain organ and use them to generate and harvest new organs that are entirely functioning.

Cure for Diseases — therapeutic cloning allows a resultant embryo to grow for days, where the stem cells could be extracted and grown into human tissue for treatments of certain diseases.

Question 30

Criteria	Mark
• Diagram identifies, stimulus, receptor, transmission, effector, response, and negativity of mechanism and return to homeostasis	3
• Diagram identifies, stimulus, receptor, transmission, effector, response, AND/OR negativity of mechanism AND/OR return to homeostasis	2
• Diagram identifies, stimulus, receptor, transmission, effector, response, OR negativity of mechanism OR return to homeostasis	1

Suggested answer:

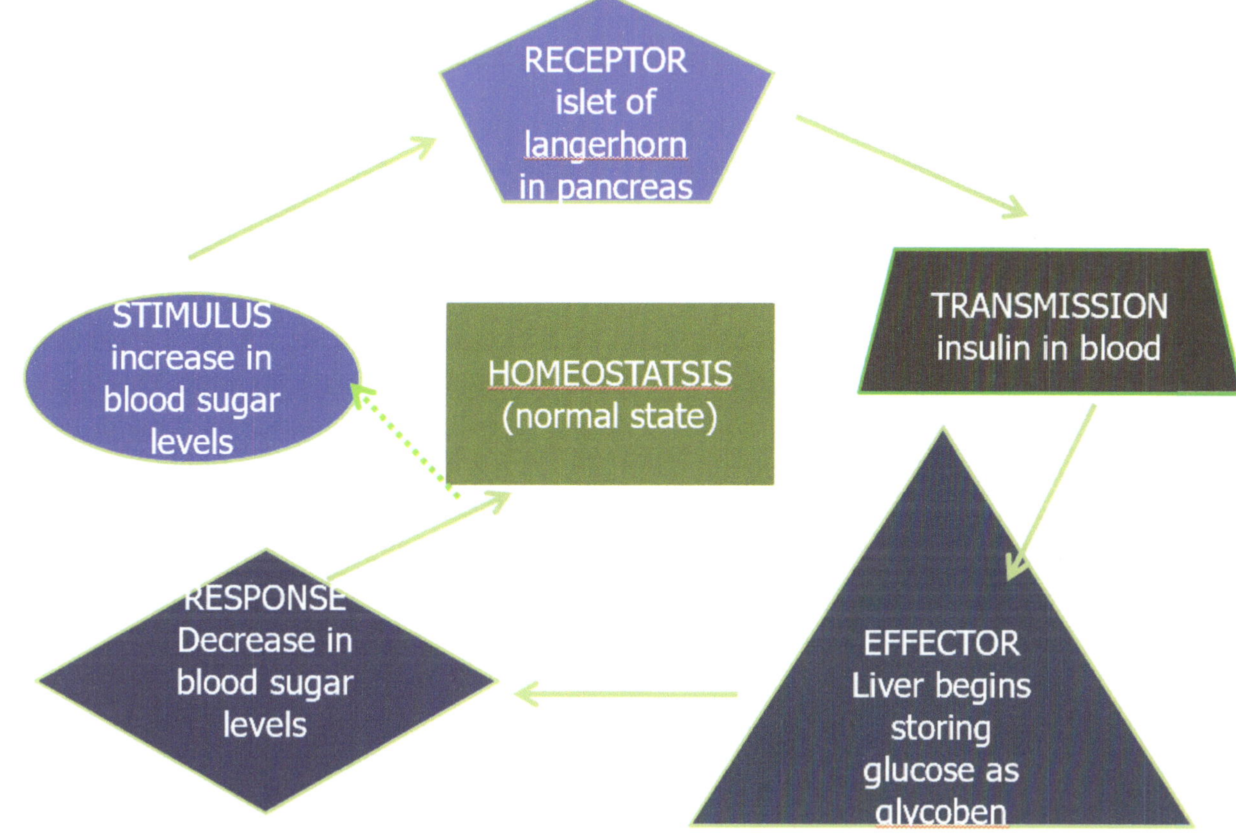

Question 31

Criteria	Mark
• Describes the technique of Recombinant DNA technology: use of plasmid and use of same restriction enzymes and identification of DNA recombining with use of Ligase, give uses a detailed accurate agricultural example	6
• Describes the technique of Recombinant DNA technology: use of plasmid and use of restriction enzymes, identification of DNA recombining AND/OR use of enzyme, give uses an accurate agricultural example	5–4
• Describes the technique of Recombinant DNA technology: use of restriction enzymes AND/OR identification of DNA recombination AND/OR give uses an outline of an agricultural example	2–3
• Some relevant information	1

Suggested answer:

Bt cotton is a transgenic crop that has been genetically modified to contain genes that produce proteins that kills the main pest of the cotton plant. These genes are first isolated from the soil bacterium Bacillus thuringiensis and removed using restriction enzymes. These same restriction enzymes are used to cut a plasmid found in the Agrobacterium tumefaciens in order for these complementary DNA cut ends to bind, with the enzyme Ligase. Thus the genes for pest resistance are now incorporated into the DNA of the plasmid in A. tunefaciens, this bacteria has the ability to transfer a plasmid into plants cells. By culturing the transformed A. tunefaciens, with plant tissue, the recombinant plasmid can move from the bacteria into the plant cells and be placed into the chromosome of the plants. These altered plant cells can then be grown in tissue culture, where the resulting plants now produce the protein that kills the main pest of the cotton plant thus reducing the need for pesticide use when producing cotton.

Question 32

Criteria	Marks
• Shows a clear and coherent understanding of the concepts • Provides an extensive analysis of the main phases in fertilisation • Gives specific examples of how the phases are important to the species continuing	7–8
• Provides an extensive analysis of the main phases in fertilisation • Gives specific examples of how the phases are important to the species continuing	5–6
• Outlines the main phases in fertilisation • Gives examples of how the phases are important to the species continuing	3–4
• Outlines the main phases in fertilisation	2
• Some relevant information	1

Suggested answer:
Fertilisation — is the fusion of gametes to form a new organism of the same species. This process involves a sperm fusing with an ovum, which eventually leads to the development of an embryo.

Implantation — occurs when the embryo reaches the blastocyst stage, approximately five to six days after fertilization,

Hormonal control of pregnancy — following conception, a new embryo sends a signal to the mother, in the form of human chorionic gonadotropin (hCG) which passes through the mother's blood to the ovaries to regulate the levels of the oestrogen and progesterone.

Birth in mammals — the process is initiated by hormones which cause the muscular walls of the uterus to contract. When this occurs, the foetus is expelled.

Question 33

Criteria	Marks
• Clearly and coherently compares and contrasts the two processes • Gives specific examples for each term to support the answer	6
• Compares and contrasts the two processes • Gives examples for each term to support the answer	4–5
• Compares and contrasts the two processes OR • Gives examples for each term to support the answer	2–3
• Some relevant information	1

Suggested answer:

Vaccination is the exposure to a weakened or dead strain of the pathogen, part of a pathogen or its membrane where an antigen is present. It is injected or orally administered into the patient's body to help their immune system adapt to the pathogen and ultimately remember it. The immune system remembers the antigen on the specific pathogen and memory cells remain to fight the pathogen if reinfection occurs. Immunisation is when the body is able to fight a pathogen and stop a disease caused by the pathogen to ever occur. To achieve immunisation, a person has to be exposed to the pathogen and win the fight against it. The vaccine stimulates your immune system so that it can recognise the disease and protects you from future infection, that means you become immune to the infection.

Question 34 (a)

Criteria	Mark
• Correct identification of both endo and ectotherm and gives valid justification for each choice	3
• Correct identification of both endo and ectotherm and gives valid justification for one choice	2
• Correct identification of BOTH endo and ectotherm	1

Suggested answer:

Lines A & C are ectotherms and B is an endotherm. Lines A & C shows the external temperature influences the internal temperature, thus an ecotherm, while in Line B the external temperature does not influence internal temperature and thus an endotherm.

Question 34 (b)

Criteria	Mark
• Correct named adaptation for both ecto and endotherm, with link to impact on thermoregulation for both ecto and endotherm.	4
• Correct named adaptation for both ecto and endotherm, with link to impact on thermoregulation for either ecto and endotherm	3
• Describes an adaptation for both endo and ecotherm.	2
• States an adaptation for either endo or ectotherm	1

Suggested answer:
An ectotherm will show the behavioural adaptation of basking in the sun to increase their body temperature in colder temperatures. An endotherm may have a structural adaptation of large hairless ears to radiate excess heat from to reduce body temperature in hot environments.

Question 35

Criteria	Mark
• Detailed description of protein structure and description of function of named proteins	5
• Detailed description of protein structure and identification of function of named proteins	4
• Outline of protein structure and description of function of named proteins	3
• Outline of protein structure and identification of function of named proteins	2
• Some relevant information	1

Suggested answer:
Proteins are built by joining amino acids into chains, called polypeptides, which can themselves form proteins or join with other polypeptides to form proteins. This primary amino acid chain, fold and coils into a secondary structure, which continues to fold forming a compact tertiary structure (polypeptides), the quaternary structure is formed when two or more polypeptides join creating a single functional protein. Due to the specific nature of the protein formation, they perform very specific roles, such as enzymes to control chemical reactions, transport to control the movement of material into, out of and around cells, and immunological proteins such as antibodies to recognise foreign material.

Mapping Grid

Section I

Q	Marks	Content	Syllabus Outcomes
1	1	Homeostasis	(8.1.1)
2	1	Fertilisation	(5.1.1)
3	1	Mitosis	(5.1.1)
4	1	DNA Synthesis	(5.3.2)
5	1	Mutations & DNA	(6.1.1 and 6.1.3)
6	1	Cell Structure	(8.1.2)
7	1	Cell Structure & Data	(8.1.2 and WS4)
8	1	Genetic Technology	(6.2.1)
9	1	Genetic Variation	(5.4.2)
10	1	Genetic Technology	(6.3.4)
11	1	Genetics	(6.3.2)
12	1	Allele Frequency	(5.4.3)
13	1	Alleles	(6.1.6)
14	1	Disease Transmission	(7.1.1)
15	1	Immune System	(7.3.2)
16	1	mRNA sequencing	(6.1.2)
17	1	Immune Response	(7.3.7)
18	1	Disease Prevention	(8.4.1)
19	1	Non-infectious diseases	(8.2.1)
20	1	Non-infectious diseases & data	(WS 4)

Section II

Q	Marks	Content	Syllabus Outcomes
21	3	DNA Replication	(8.1.2)
22	4	Immune Response	(7.3.2)
23	6	Nondisjunction of DNA	(6.1.2)
24	8	Biomedical technology	(8.5.1)
25	6	Genetic technology	(6.3.5)
26	3	Infectious disease	(7.3.2)
27	3	Chromosomal Errors	(6.1.2)
28	5	Infectious disease	(6.3.3)
29	7	Cloning	(6.3.3)
30	3	Feedback mechanisms	(8.1.1)
31	6	Transgenic organisms	(6 3.4)
32	8	Mammalian reproduction	(5.1.2)
33	6	Vaccination	(7. 3. 2 and 5)
34	5	Homeostasis	(5 .2 .1 and 2)
35	5	Proteins	(5.3.3)

2021 YEAR 11 EXAMINATION	
BIOLOGY	
General Instructions	• Reading time – 5 minutes • Working time – 2 hours • Write using black pen • Draw diagrams using pencil • Calculators approved by NESA may be used
Total marks: 75	Section I – 20 marks (pages 2–8) • Attempt Questions 1–20 • Allow about 35 minutes for this section
	Section II – 55 marks (pages 10–36) • Attempt Questions 21–30 • Allow about 1 hours and 25 minutes for this section

Section I

20 marks
Attempt Questions 1–20
Allow about 35 minutes for this section

Use the multiple-choice answer sheet for Questions 1–20.

1. Which of the following are all features of unicellular organisms:

A.	Single cell	Mostly procaryotic	Mostly asexual, clonal reproduction
B.	Many cells	eukaryotic	Mostly sexual reproduction
C.	Single cell	Mostly procaryotic	Mostly sexual reproduction
D.	Single cell	All eukaryotic	Mostly asexual, clonal reproduction

2. Multicellular organisms can be organised into the following levels of complexity. Starting with organelles, which of the following moves from less complex to more complex

   A. Organelles → Cells → Organs → Tissues → Systems
   B. Organelles → Organs → Cells → Tissues → System
   C. Organelles → Cells → Tissues → Organs → System
   D. Organelles → Organs → Tissues → Cells → Systems

3. How do sunken stomata assist acacia to survive in their environment?

   A. They increase transpiration.
   B. They increase the surface-area-to-volume ratio of the leaf.
   C. They reduce the surface-area-to-volume ratio of the leaf.
   D. They reduce the difference in water potential.

4. Darwin's ideas on evolution and natural selection rely on which major assumption?

   A. All species are related
   B. The environment changes a species.
   C. Variation must exist in a population.
   D. All living things are affected by their environment.

Below is a graph showing the relative abundance of Mangrove Species A, B and C along a transect line. Refer to this graph when answering Questions 5 & 6

Relative abundance of Mangrove A, B and C

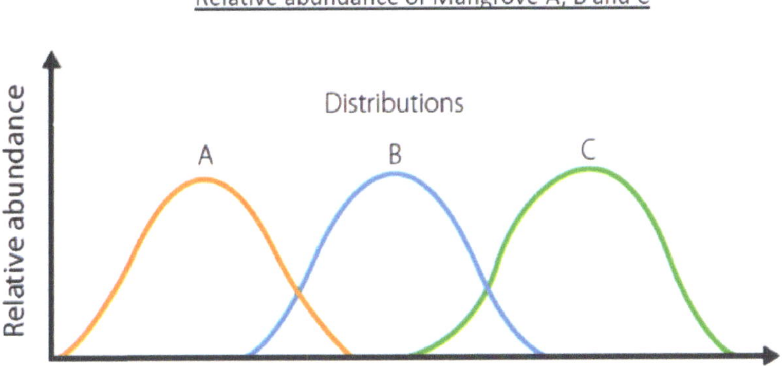

https://slideplayer.com/slide/5697316

5. Choose the option that best describes the abundance of mangroves.
   A. Mangrove species A is highest in abundance close to the sea.
   B. Mangrove species C is highest in abundance close to the sea.
   C. Mangrove species B is highest in abundance close to the sea.
   D. All mangrove species are found close to the sea.

6. What inference can be made about Mangrove species C?
   A. It is the most common species found.
   B. It is the most tolerant of saline conditions, followed by Species B.
   C. It is more abundant than species A & B.
   D. It is evenly distributed.

7. How are populations with low genetic biodiversity affected by a changing environment?
   A. They can change to suit the changes in the environment.
   B. They run the risk of extinction even if their numbers increase.
   C. They run the risk of extinction only if their numbers decrease.
   D. They can survive if they can adapt to the changes.

8. The diagram below shows a periwinkle which lives on the rocky shoreline of our coast. It has a hard shell which stops it drying out at low tide and will use its muscular foot to move into small rock pools when the tide is low. It has gills which allow it to extract oxygen from water.

The adaptations which are mentioned above, which allow the periwinkle to survive, could be classified as:

A. Behavioural and Structural
B. Structural only
C. Behavioural, Structural and Physiological
D. Physiological and Behavioural

9. Which of the following are the building blocks of protein?

A. Nucleotides
B. Triglycerides
C. Amino Acids
D. Monosaccharides

10. Which of the following best describes the activity of enzymes and temperature?

A. At low temperatures, the rate of enzyme activity will be the highest.
B. At high temperatures, the rate of enzyme activity will be the highest.
C. At room temperature, the rate of enzyme activity is at its optimum.
D. At very high temperatures, the rate of enzyme activity decreases.

11. The process of anaerobic cellular respiration is different to aerobic respiration because it produces?

A. Carbon Dioxide
B. Glucose
C. Alcohol and/or lactic acid
D. Energy

12. Which of the following technologies/techniques NOT used to collect evidence when determining changes in the past environment?

    A. Radiometric Dating
    B. Stereomicroscope
    C. Ice Core Drilling
    D. Gas Analysis

13. A student wanted to know how effective it would be to spray the weeds on the school oval. What would be the best method to use to measure the number of weeds on the oval before and after spraying with weed killer?

    A. Transect Study
    B. Random Quadrats
    C. Complete count
    D. Capture - mark - recapture

14. Which of the following is the most correct regarding the distribution of a species in an Ecosystem?

    A. It informs biologists about the number of organisms in a population.
    B. It is determined by the availability of biotic and abiotic factors.
    C. It describes the feeding relationships in an ecosystem.
    D. It remains unchanged over a period.

15. Data collection on the distribution and abundance of wild Tasmanian devils is important in order to manage the spread of Devil Facial Tumour Disease. This is mainly because:

    A. This data allows scientists to identify the cause of the disease.
    B. The virus is airborne and spreads faster in overcrowded devil populations.
    C. It will allow scientists to manage the ecological impacts of reduced numbers of devils.
    D. Scientists want to collect infected devils and move them to disease free locations.

16. Trilobites are an aquatic organism that diversified quickly during the Cambrian period. Their fossils reflect continuous change in their structures. What type of evolution is evident in trilobites?

    A. Gradualism
    B. Microevolution
    C. Punctuated equilibrium
    D. Convergent evolution

17. Darwin noted observations about the antlion in his journal:

    Ant lions to that of England: 'I observed a conical pitfall of a Lion-Ant: a fly fell in and immediately disappeared; ... without doubt this predacious lava [sic] belongs to the same genus, but to a different species from the European one ... Now what would the Disbeliever say to this? Would any two workmen ever hit on so beautiful, so simple and yet so artificial a contrivance? I cannot think so. The one hand has worked over the whole world'.

    How did Darwin explain the similarities in the behaviour of antlions?

    A. They evolved in similar environments.
    B. The displayed convergent evolution.
    C. They belonged to the same genus and species.
    D. They belonged to the same genus but different species.

18. Which of the following best describes how the sclerophyll plants evolved?

    A. The change from a warm dry to a cool moist climate led to a decrease in rainforest and an increase in the sclerophyll forest.
    B. The change from a cool moist to a warm dry climate and the increase in bushfires has led to the growth of the sclerophyll forest and a decline of the rainforest.
    C. The frequent droughts across the east coast of Australia has led to an increase in both the The frequent bushfires and changing weather conditions has led to an increase in both the rainforest and the sclerophyll forest.

19. Many infectious disease outbreaks are due to an alteration in the balance of biotic and abiotic factors in an ecosystem. This is because:

    A. The pathogen changes to become more contagious and moves through populations faster.
    B. The hosts may have lowered disease resistance due to stresses from the environment.
    C. The pathogen develops new ways to cause disease due to a change in its genetic structure.
    D. There is a decrease in the breeding sites for vectors of the disease.

20. Horseshoe crabs have changed very little in the past 445 million years. This is most likely due to the fact:

A. they were fully evolved.
B. they did not produce enough offspring for natural selection to occur.
C. they were able to live both in the sea and on land.
D. there was little change in their environment.

2021 PRELIMINARY EXAMINATION	
Biology **Section II Answer Booklet**	Centre Number Student Number

55 marks
Attempt Questions 21–30
Allow about 1 hours and 25 minutes for this section

Instructions	• Write your Centre Number and Student Number at the top of this page • Answer the questions in the spaces provided. These spaces provide guidance for the expected length of response. • Show all relevant working in questions involving calculations.

Please turn over

Question 21 (3 marks)

The diagram below is a scaled image of a cell under a microscope.

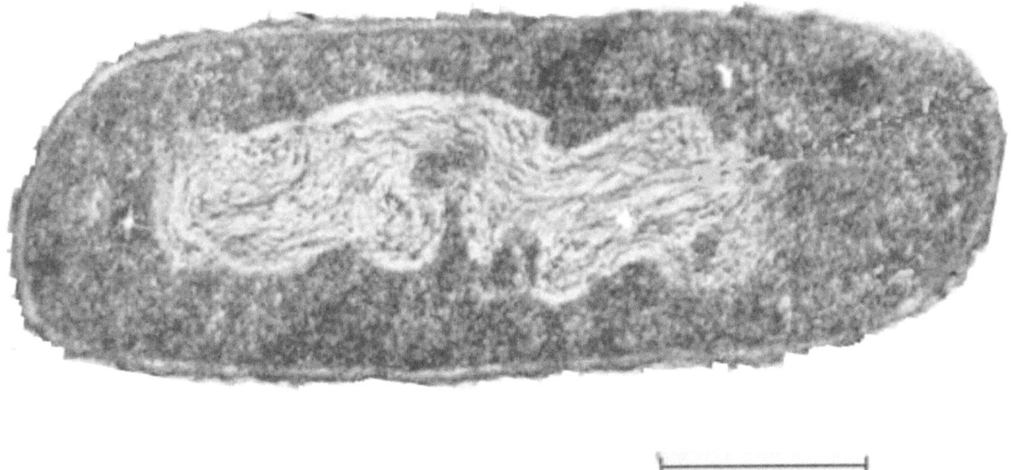

1 μm

(a) Estimate the length of this cell using the scale provided. 1

....

....

....

(b) Label 2 distinctive features on the diagram above that would determine whether this cell is prokaryotic or eukaryotic. 2

Question 22 (2 marks)

(a) What is the function of the nephron in a kidney? 1

....

....

....

(b) Identify two chemicals that are removed from the blood by the kidney. 1

....

....

....

Question 23 (8 marks)

A student conducted an experiment to determine if the surface area to volume ratio of jelly agar affects the time it takes for a chemical to diffuse into the centre of a jelly. The graph below shows the results of his experiment.

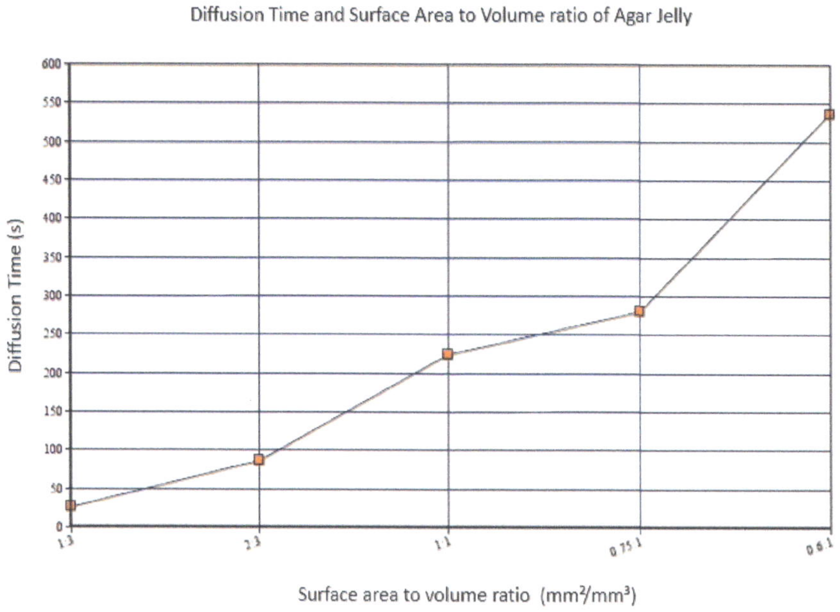

Diffusion Time and Surface Area to Volume ratio of Agar Jelly

Diffusion Time (s)

600
550
500
450
400
350
300
250
200
150
100
50
0

1:3 2:3 1:1 0.75:1 0.6:1

Surface area to volume ratio (mm^2/mm^3)

(a) Using the trend shown in the graph, justify the following statement: The exchange of materials between a cell and its environment depends on the surface area to volume ratio. 3

....
....
....
....
....
....
....
....
....

(b) There are specialised microscopic structures called alveoli that are important for gas exchange in mammals. Explain how this structure aids in the exchange of gases required for cell requirements. 2

....
....
....
....
....
....

(c) Not all materials required by the cell can diffuse across a cell membrane. Explain why active transport is important by referring to a named molecule required by a cell. 3

....
....
....
....
....
....
....
....
....

Question 24 (8 marks)

Complete the table below which compares two essential processes which take place in autotrophs and heterotrophs.

PROCESS	PHOTOSYNTHESIS	RESPIRATION
Organelle where process occurs		
When the process occurs		
Substances produced		
Substances required for the process		

Question 25 (6 marks)

Compare the structure and functions of the human circulatory system and transport systems in plants. 6

....
....
....
....
....
....
....
....
....
....
....
....
....
....
....
....
....
....

Question 26 (7 marks)

Antibiotics (such as *MRSA, VRE* & *FQRP*), also called antibacterial, are a type of drug used in the treatment and prevention of bacterial infections. They may either kill or inhibit the growth of bacteria.

Antibiotics revolutionized medicine in the 20th century. However, their effectiveness and easy access have also led to their overuse, prompting some bacterial species to develop resistance.

Use the graph below to answer the questions that follow.

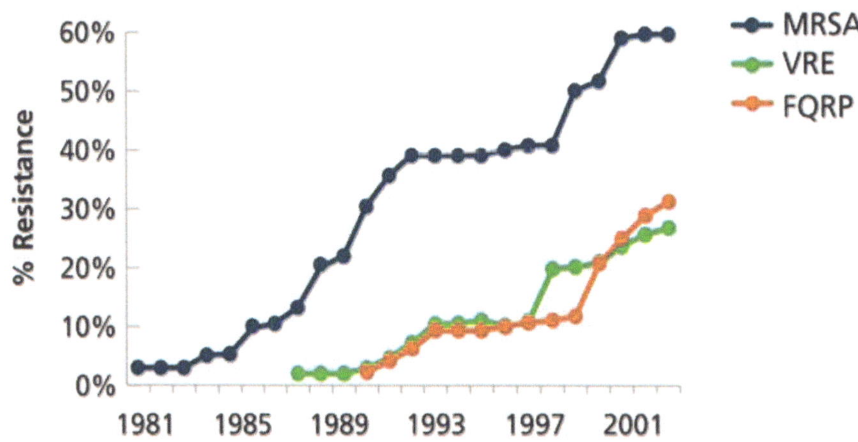

https://www.silverbook.org/fact/increase-in-antibiotic-resistance/

(a) Describe the trend shown in the graph. 2

....
....
....
....
....
....

(b) The development of antibiotic resistant 'super bugs' such as the bacterium *MRSA*, *VRE* and *FQRP* is a real concern. 5

Explain the development of a 'Super Bug' through Darwin's theory of natural selection.

....
....
....
....
....
....
....
....
....
....
....
....
....
....
....
....

Question 27 (4 marks)

Scientists have been able to reconstruct a geological time scale which shows the course of change of geological and fossil deposits and link this to evolutionary changes.

(a) Explain how one piece of evidence has been used to provide evidence of past changes in ecosystems. 3

....
....
....
....
....
....
....
....

(b) A Palaeontologist in Antarctica discovered a fossil that he suspects is the same fossil found in a town in New South Wales. Identify a digital technology that can be used to validate this discovery. 1

....

....

Question 28 (5 marks)

A student counted the number of waratah anemones found in a 1 m^2 quadrat placed along 5 different transect lines at his local rock platform.

On each transect line the quadrats were placed 5 m, 10 m, 15 m, and 20 m from the low tide shoreline.

An example of one of his transect lines is listed below.

⊟ = Quadrat

Low Tide Mark ________⊟________⊟________⊟________⊟ High Tide Mark

Water 5 m 10 m 15 m 20 m

The table below shows the data he collected along the 5 transect lines.

(a) Complete the table by working out the averages at each distance. **2**
Number of Waratah Anemones found in 1 m^2 quadrats along each transect

Distance from shore (m)	Transect 1	Transect 2	Transect 3	Transect 4	Transect 5	Average Number
5	40	30	38	41	51	
10	12	18	6	12	9	
15	8	12	16	6	3	
20	0	0	0	0	0	

(b) In the space below graph the results to show how the abundance of waratah anemones changes as you move away from the low tide water mark. (Use the average you calculated for part a) 3

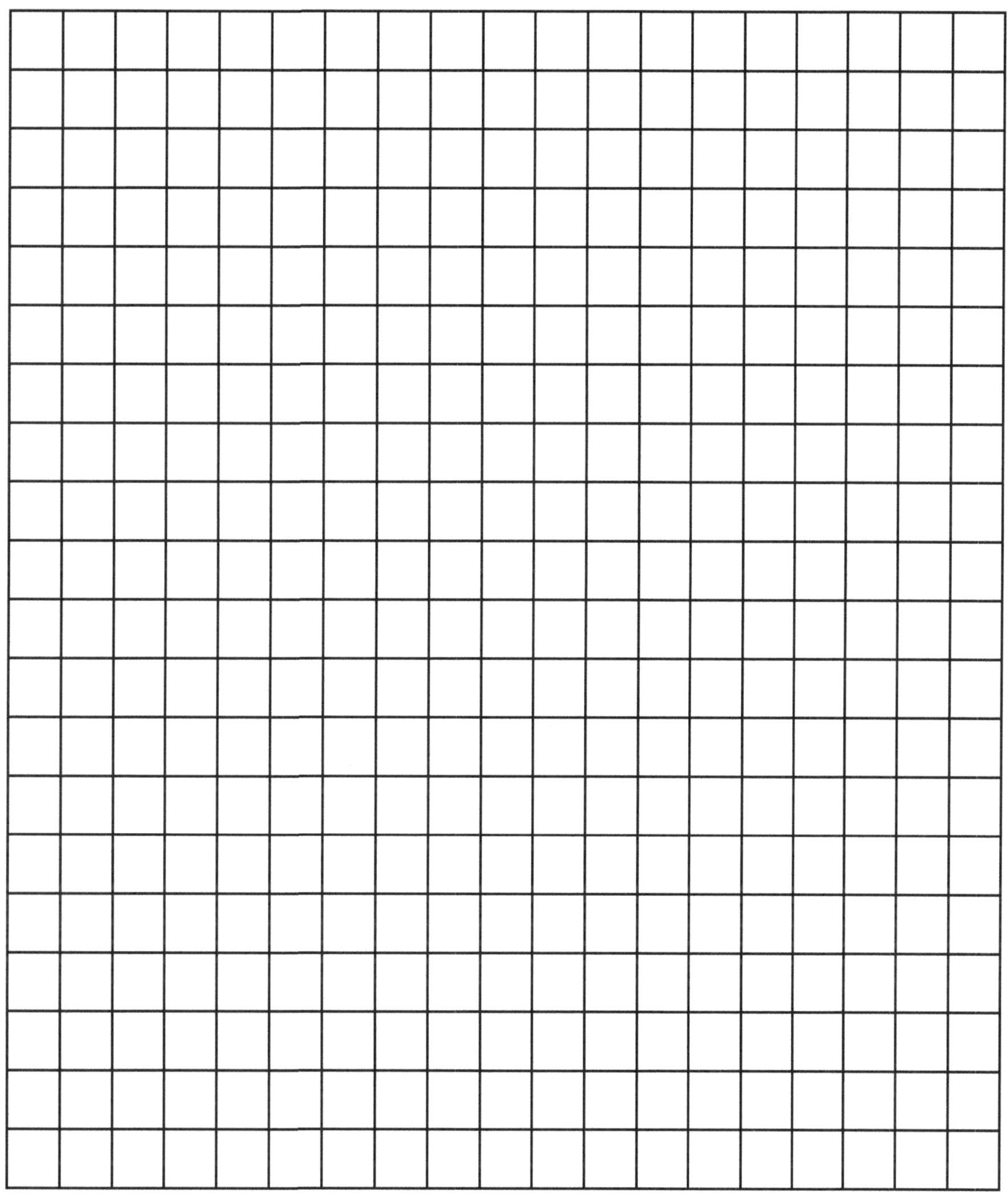

Distance from shore (m)

Question 29 (5 marks)

Since the introduction of Cane Toads into Australia, there has been a rapid evolution in both the Cane Toad and a few native animals. Overtime, a large population of fast-moving Cane toads were able to establish themselves across the Northern Territory and Western Australia.

The Cane toads produce a toxin that can kill many of our native predators such as Red-Bellied Black Snakes that have larger heads. Recent evidence suggests that there has been an increase in the population of Red-belly Black Snakes that have smaller heads. The diet of the smaller headed, red-bellied black snakes consists mainly of slugs and earthworms, but will also eat snails, pill bugs, insect larvae, and small salamanders rather than frogs and Cane toads.

Figure 1 shows the number of Cane Toads and Native Frogs consumed by Red-Bellied Black snakes in an area and the time Cane Toads were present in that area for.

Figure 1.

Type of Prey Offered	**Percentage of Snakes from Each Area That ate the Native Frog vs. Cane Toad**	
	Area with Cane Toads Present for 40-60 Years	**Area with No Cane Toads**
Native Frog	100	100
Cane Toad	0	50

Using the information and the data above, assess the impact of a selection pressure on the evolution, abundance and the ecological niche of the Red Bellied black snakes mentioned above. 5

....

....

....

....

....

....

....

....

....

....

Question 30 (7 marks)
In aquaculture, the Red Sea Bream is one of Japan's most important commercial fish. However, since the mid-20th century, there has been a significant decline in this fish population.

The seagrass beds in the shallow coastal waters around Japan are suggested to be an important nursery for many fish including the red sea bream since they provide the juveniles with habitat complexity as well as serve as a feeding ground.

However, the seagrass bed population has also been on a decline around the world. The sea grass relies on sunlight exposure; however, these can be shaded by algae. Heavy rain increases the volume of freshwater runoff from the rivers which causes increased turbidity and sedimentation in coastal waters. Increased run-off has increased nitrogen and phosphorus levels in the water leading to algae blooms.

Seagrass beds have also been on a decline due damage to the leaves, stems and roots by objects in the water.

(a) The capture recapture method is a technique commonly used to determine the size of population of the Red Sea Bream collected in a Japanese fish farm. The table below shows the number of Red Sea bream that were tagged from each sample off the coast of Japan. The original number of Red Sea Bream caught and tagged was 25. 3

Sample #	**Number of tagged fish in the sample**	**Total sample size**
1	3	8
2	3	9
3	4	12
4	5	9
5	5	17
Average	__________	__________

Question continued on next page

(i) Calculate the average number of tagged fish in each sample and the average total sample size. Write your answer in the table above. 1

(ii) Using the data in the table above and the formula below, estimate the total population of the Red Sea Bream. Note: your answer must be rounded off to a whole number. 2

Total population

$$= \frac{\textit{number of caught tagged in original sample} \times \textit{average number caugh in each samples}}{\textit{average number of tagged in each samples}}$$

....
....
....
....

(b) Identify TWO human activities and explain how these activities may have affected the relationship between the SeaGrass bed and the Red Sea Bream. 4

....
....
....
....
....
....
....
....
....
....
....
....

Marking Guidelines LMC
Biology Preliminary Examination 2021

Section I: Multiple-choice Answer Key

Question	Answer
1	A
2	C
3	D
4	C
5	B
6	B
7	B
8	C
9	C
10	D
11	C
12	B
13	B
14	B
15	C
16	A
17	D
18	B
19	B
20	D

Section II

Question 21 (a)

Criteria	Marks
• Correctly estimates the length using the provided scale	1

Sample answer:
5 micrometers

Question 21 (b)

Criteria	Marks
• Identify and label both the nucleotide and the cell membrane	2
• Identifies only one feature on the cell	1

Sample answer:

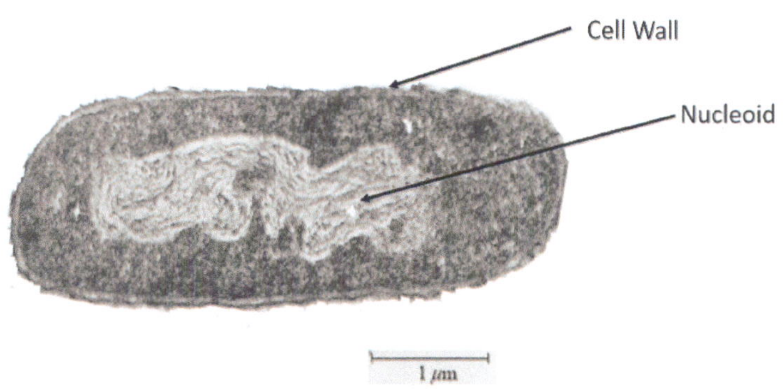

Question 22 (a)

Criteria	Marks
• Accurately describes the function of the nephron	1

Sample answer:
A nephron is a functional unit in the kidney that regulates water and soluble substances by filtering the blood

Question 22 (b)

Criteria	Marks
• Correctly identifies 2 chemicals removed from the blood by the kidney	1

Sample answer:
Any of the following urea, salt, water, vitamins, amino acids,glucose

Question 23 (a)

Criteria	Marks
• Justified using the graph that the environment depends on the surface area to volume ratio.	3
• using the graph that the environment depends on the surface area to volume ratio.	2
• Mentions aspects of surface area to volume ratio	1

Sample answer:
As shown in the graph, as the surface area to volume ratio increases, the time of diffusion decreases which means there is a slower exchange of materials between a cell and its environment as the cell size increases

Question 23 (b)

Criteria	Marks
• Explains that alveoli are important for gas exchange in mammals.	2
• Mentions alveoli as a structure needed for gaseous exchange	1

Sample answer:
The alveoli has thin walls to allow oxygen to cross into the surrounding capillaries from inside the alveoli and to allow carbon dioxide to exit the surrounding capillaries and into the alveoli.

Question 23 (c)

Criteria	Marks
• Explains that active transport is important by referring to a named molecule required by a cell.	3
• Mentions active transport is important and required by a cell.	2
• Mentions active transport is important to a cell.	1

Sample answer:
Active transport requires the use of energy to transport molecules against their concentration gradient. An example of this is glucose, which is important in cellular respiration.

Question 24

Criteria	Marks
• All 8 entries are in the table	8
• 7 correct entries are in the table	7
• 6 correct entries are in the table	6
• 5 correct entries are in the table	5
• 4 correct entries are in the table	4
• 3 correct entries are in the table	3
• 2 correct entries are in the table	2
• 1 correct entry	1

Sample answer:

PROCESS	PHOTOSYNTHESIS	RESPIRATION
Organelle where process occurs	**Chloroplast**	**Mitochondria**
When the process occurs	**Daylight Hours**	**All the time**
Substances produced	**Oxygen + Glucose**	**ATP + Carbon dioxide**
Substances required for the process	**Carbon Dioxide + Water (light)**	**Oxygen + Glucose**

Question 25

Criteria	Marks
• Compares by outlining the structure and function of Arteries, Veins and Capillaries in Humans to the structure and function of Xylem and phloem tissue in plants	6
• Outlines the structure and function of Arteries, Veins and Capillaries in Humans to the structure and function of Xylem and Phloem tissue in plants	5
• Outlines the structure and function of some blood vessels and xylem or phloem tissue	4
• Outlines the structure **OR** function of some blood vessels and xylem or phloem tissue	3
• Outlines the structure **OR** function of a blood vessels and xylem or phloem tissue	2
• Outlines the structure **OR** function of a blood vessels OR xylem or phloem tissue	1

Sample answer:
The human circulatory system is a closed system made up of a network of Arteries Veins and capillaries which transport nutrients (glucose), water and oxygen to all living cells in the body. These substances are found in blood.

The Heart is the organ which pumps blood around the body. Arteries transport oxygenated blood from the heart to other body organs and veins return deoxygenated blood back to the heart. The arteries have thick muscular walls transporting blood under pressure where veins contain valves to prevent blood flowing backwards.

Capillaries are only very thin so materials can diffuse into the cells where nutrients are needed.

In plants water and sugars move in different ways. Water enters through the roots and is transported through xylem vessels and exits through the leaves (the cells are not living but have rings of lignified tissue which aids strength to the vessels). The movement is in one direction and the adhesive forces between water molecules and the narrow xylem walls draws water up the stem, as it evaporates from the leaf surface.

Sugars are made in the leaf (via photosynthesis) and transported through phloem vessels. The phloem vessels are separated by sieve plates and have companion cells next to them. These cells transport sugars up and down the plant to where they are required.

So the two systems are similar in the way they move nutrients to living cells; they are very different in their structure and way they function.

Question 26 (a)

Criteria	Marks
• Identifies the trend in the graph • Supports it with data	2
• Identifies the trend **OR** • Provides relevant data from graph	1

Sample answer:
Since the introduction of antibiotics MRSA in 1981, its resistance has increased from almost 2% to 60%. Similar trend can be seen for the other two antibiotics (VRE & FQRP) since their introduction in 1987and 1990, respectively.

Question 26 (b)

Criteria	Marks
• Demonstrates a thorough understanding of Darwin's theory of natural selection • Relates theory of natural selection to the evolution of antibiotic resistance and uses data from graph.	5
• Demonstrates extensive understanding of Darwins theory of natural selection • Relates theory of natural selection to the evolution of antibiotic resistance **OR** • Links aspects of natural selection to antibiotic resistance with the support of data.	3-4
• Outlines some steps of Darwin's theory of natural selection • Briefly relates theory of natural selection to evolution of antibiotic resistance **OR** supports	2
• Provides some relevant information about theory of natural selection	1

Sample answer:
The starting point is a large bacterial population mainly consisting of bacteria that are susceptible to antibiotics and a couple of bacteria that are antibiotic-resistant by chance. When an antibiotic like MRSA is added, which kills most of the susceptible bacteria in the population who are susceptible to this selective pressure, while the resistant bacteria survives and reproduces. Only the resistant bacteria will continue to proliferate in the presence of the antibiotic and increases in number over time passing its favourable characteristic to the following generation. This continues over many generations, eventually resulting in a population of mainly resistant bacteria. Example, around 60% of the population of MRSA, as seen in the graph, has become resistant to antibiotics after 20 years.

Question 27 (a)

Criteria	Marks
Student describes how the radiometric dating procedure or the relative dating procedure can determine how these two fossils are the same age and from this explains how these fossils prove how Australia and Antarctica were once joined together.	3
Student identifies the technology/technique of radiometric dating procedure and uses this to describe how these fossils prove Australia and Antarctica were once joined together.	2
Student identifies the technology/technique of radiometric dating procedure **OR** Outlines how these fossils show Australia and Antarctica were once joined together.	1

Sample answer:
Geological evidence such as banded iron formations contains a large amount of iron oxide. This iron oxide would have formed when an increase in the oxygen concentration in the area over time, therefore proving that the environment changed from an anaerobic to an aerobic one.

Question 27 (b)

Criteria	Marks
• Identify a digital technology that can be used to validate this discovery of fossil evidence on different continents	1

Sample answer:
Use of digital reconstruction of the then existing continents using an open source software model that can go back in time to the early days of the Earth such as version 2.0 of GPlates.

Question 28 (a)

Criteria	Marks
• All averages correctly calculated	2
• 1-2 averages correctly calculated	1

Sample answer:

Number of Waratah Anemones found in 1m^2 quadrats along each transect

Distance from shore (m)	Transect 1	Transect 2	Transect 3	Transect 4	Transect 5	Average Number
5	40	30	38	41	51	**40**
10	12	18	6	12	9	**11**
15	8	12	16	6	3	**9**
20	0	0	0	0	0	**0**

Question 28 (a)

Criteria	Marks
• Y axis correctly labelled, correct scale, correct plotting and line graph	3
• Y axis correctly labelled, correct scale, correct plotting	2
• Y axis correctly labelled OR correct scale OR correct plotting	1

Sample answer:

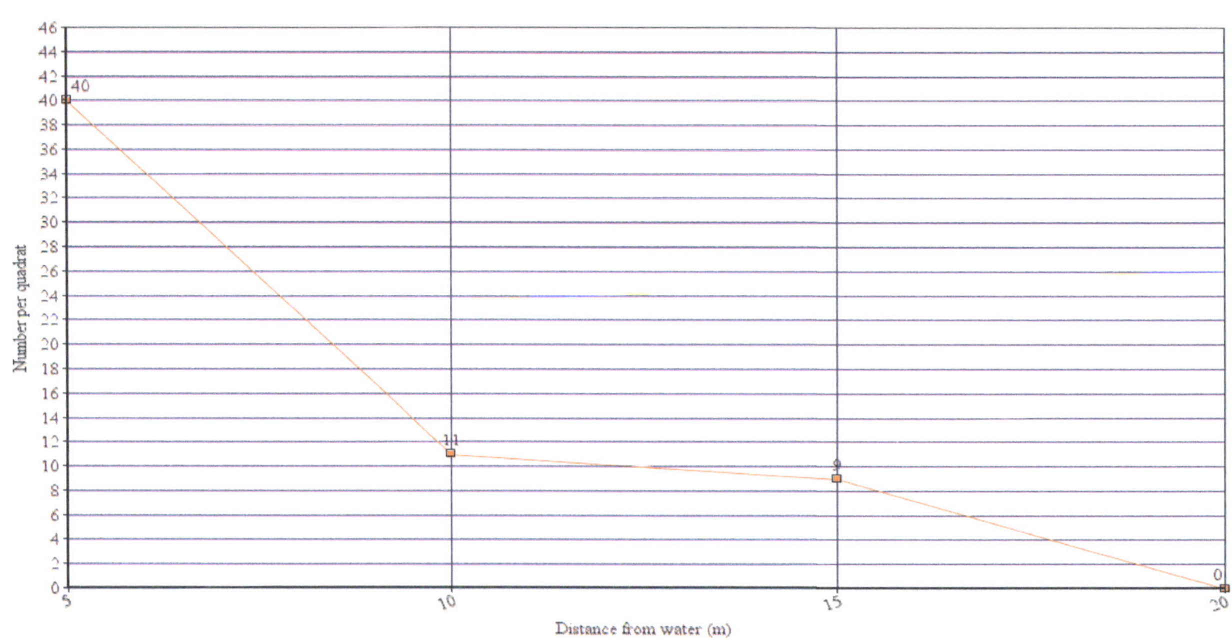

Question 29

Criteria	Marks
• An informed assessment is made on the impact of the selection pressure on the evolution, abundance and the ecological niche of the Red-bellied black snake with reference to the information and the data from figure 1. • Student describes how the process of evolution would have procured among the population of the Red-Bellied Black Snake.	5
• An assessment is made on the impact of the selection pressure on the evolution, abundance and the ecological niche of the Red-bellied black snake with limited reference to the information and/or the data from figure 1. • Student describes how the process of evolution would have procured among the population of the Red-Bellied Black Snake.	3-4
• Student describes how the process of evolution would have procured among the population of the Red-Bellied Black Snake. **OR** • An assessment is made on the impact two of the following with limited reference to the information provided: - Abundance - Evolution - Ecological Niche	2
• Any relevant information about either the selection pressure, abundance, ecological niche or the evolution of the red bellied black snake is provided.	1

Sample answer:

-The toxin released by the Cane toad acts as a selection pressure, where over time, the larger heading snakes that were able to consume the cane toads were killed by the toxins from the cane toad, and the snakes that had smaller head were not able to consume these toads were able to reach maturity and reproduce, this would therefore change the population of snakes to mainly a small-headed population.

-This is supported by the data, where Cane toads living in an area for longer (40-60 years) were not consumed by the snakes compared to an area where Cane toads were initially introduced. Whereas the amount of frogs consumed by snakes in either areas does not change.

This selection pressure would allow both the Cane toads and the Snakes to occupy the same niche/habitat and/or force snakes to consume smaller prey.

Question 30 (a) (i)

Criteria	Marks
• Students calculates both averages correctly.	1

Sample answer: *(Student writes their answers in the table.)*
Average number of fish tagged: 4
Average number of fish in each sample: 11

Question 30 (a) (ii)

Criteria	Marks
• Student uses the formula and their averages to get the correct estimate (whole number) of the population.	2
• Student uses the formula and their averages but obtains an incorrect answer **OR**, • Student uses the formula and their averages but obtains an answer that is not rounded off to a whole number	1

Sample answer:
Total population = 25 × 11 ÷ 4 = 68.75 which is rounded off to 69
Total population estimate is 69

Question 30 (b)

Criteria	Marks
• Student has correctly identified TWO human activities that are relevant to the information provided at the start of the question and they explain how EACH activity may have affected the relationship between the SeaGrass bed and the Red Sea Bream using cause and effect links.	4
• Student has correctly identified TWO human activities that are relevant to the information provided at the start of the question and the effect of each activity is explained mostly correctly.	3
• Student has correctly identified TWO human activities that are relevant to the information provided at the start of the question and an outcome of each activity is outlined with no cause and effect link.	2
• Any relevant information is provided.	1

Sample answer:
The use of fertiliser during agricultural practices has increased the nutrition content in waterways due to the run-off of water. This has caused algae blooms which have reduced the amount of sunlight received by sea grass beds.

The propellers from boating activities have caused the roots and stems of seagrass beds to be damaged/removed.

As a result of this the population of seagrass beds have declined. This decline means that the shelter and feeding grounds for the sea bream is taken away, resulting in the decrease in the sea bream.

Mapping Grid

Section I

Q	Marks	Content	Syllabus Outcomes
1	1	Multicellular organisms	(2.1.1)
2	1	Hierarchical organisation	(2.1.3)
3	1	Adaptations	(3.2.1)
4	1	Natural Selection	(3.4.1)
5	1	Population Dynamics	(4.1.1)
6	1	Population Dynamics	(4.1.1)
7	1	Effect of Factors on an environment	(3.1.1 and 4.1.1)
8	1	Adaptations	(3.2.1)
9	1	Cell function	(1.2.2)
10	1	Cell function	(1.2.5)
11	1	Cell function	(1.2.3)
12	1	Past Ecosystems	(4.1.1 and 4.2.2)
13	1	Population Dynamics	(4.1.1)
14	1	Effect of Factors on an environment	(3.1.1)
15	1	Future Ecosystems	(4.3.1)
16	1	Effect of Factors on an environment	(3.1.4)
17	1	Organisation of cells	(2.1.2)
18	1	Past Ecosystems	(4.2.3)
19	1	Effect of Factors on an environment	(3.1.1)
20	1	Effect of Factors on an environment	(3.1.4)

Section II

Q	Marks	Content	Syllabus Outcomes
21	3	Cell structure	(1.1.1)
22	2	Nutrient and Gas requirements	(2.2.5)
23	8	Cell function	(1.2.1)
24	8	Nutrient and Gas requirements	(2.2.6)
25	6	Transport	(2.3.3)
26	7	Evolution	(3,4.2)
27	4	Past Ecosystems	(4.2.1)
28	5	Population Dynamics	(4.1.1)
29	5	Adaptations and Past Ecosystems	(3.1.2 and 4.2.1)
30	7	Population Dynamics	(4.1.1)

2021 TRIAL HIGHER SCHOOL CERTIFICATE EXAMINATION	
Biology	
General Instructions	• Reading time – 5 minutes • Working time – 3 hours • Write using black pen • Draw diagrams using pencil • Calculators approved by NESA may be used
Total marks: 100	Section I – 20 marks (pages 2–8) • Attempt Questions 1–20 • Allow about 35 minutes for this section
	Section II – 80 marks (pages 10–25) • Attempt Questions 21–35 • Allow about 2 hours and 25 minutes for this section

Section I

20 marks
Attempt Questions 1–20
Allow about 35 minutes for this section

Use the multiple-choice answer sheet for Questions 1–20.

1. Which of the following is an asexual method of reproduction?

   A. Meiosis
   B. Budding
   C. Fertilisation in plants
   D. Mutation

2. What is one disadvantage and one advantage of sexual reproduction?

	Disadvantage	Advantage
A.	Variation	one parent required
B.	Two parents required	variation in species occurs
C.	Cloning can result from two parent cells	variation of species
D.	The same type of gametes	variation of species

3.

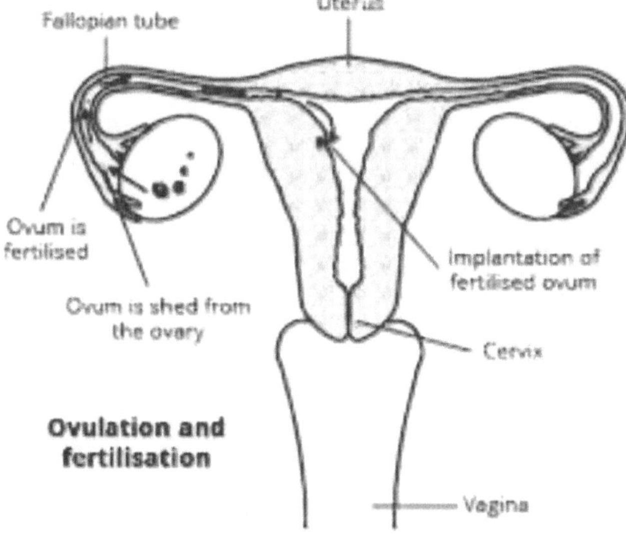

The function of the ovary is to:

A. Produce oocyte
B. Used for transporting the foetus to the uterus
C. Produce sperm cells
D. Carry the uterine lining to the uterus

4. Chargaff's rule states that there the same number of adenine bases to thymine bases and cytosine to guanine bases on the DNA strand. The DNA strand is a:

A. Single strand wound up on itself with base pairs in random order
B. Double stranded molecule with rungs formed by nitrogenous bases
C. Phosphate backbone holding up the bases on a single DNA strand
D. Complex molecule with a bi-lipid layer

5. In early 2016, there was an outbreak of food poisoning in New South Wales linked to the consumption of pre-packaged lettuce.

The Department of Health carried out an investigation of this. They found that several products tested positive for the prokaryote Salmonella anatum.

It is reasonable to say that S. anatum is:

A. a virus.
B. a prion.
C. an insect.
D. a bacterium.

6. A daily blood sample was obtained from an individual who received a single vaccination against a particular strain of the influenza virus. The individual had no prior exposure to this strain of influenza.

The graph below shows the concentration of antibodies present in the individual's blood for this strain of influenza over a period.

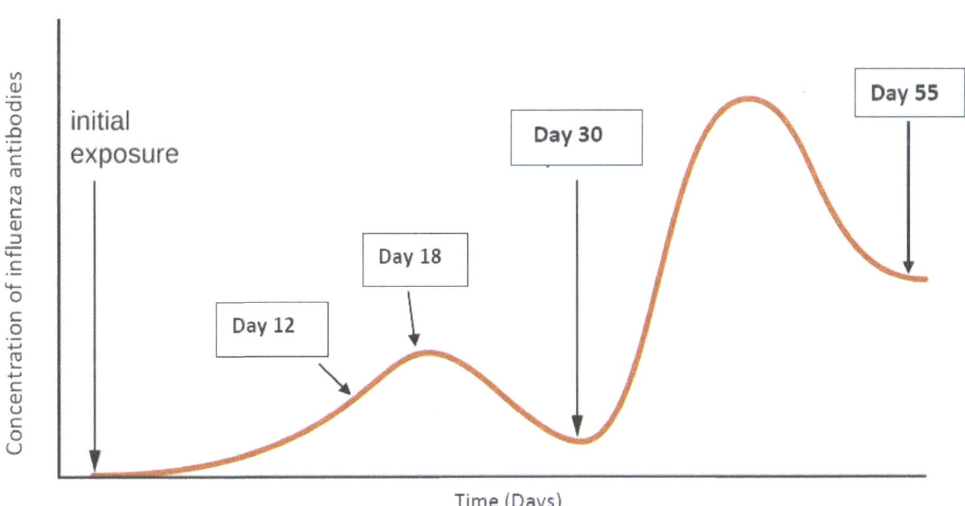

Which one of the following conclusions can be made using this data?

A. Memory B cells were activated by exposure to the same strain of the influenza virus on day 30.
B. Plasma B cells specific to this strain of influenza were most numerous on day 18.
C. Herd immunity to this particular strain of influenza was achieved by day 55.
D. The vaccination containing weakened influenza antigens occurred on day 12.

7. In the search for a malaria vaccine, scientists have focused on a protein called circumsporozoite protein (CSP).

   CSP is secreted by the malaria parasite and is present on its surface.

   For the vaccination to work, the scientists want CSP to act as

   A. an antigen.
   B. an allergen.
   C. an antibody.
   D. a complement protein.

8. What simple chemical in a living thing is the fundamental unit of protein synthesis

   A. Amino acids
   B. Carbohydrates
   C. Lipids
   D. Vitamins and Minerals

9. A punnett square is a valuable diagram used in genetics. The use of this diagram is to:

   A. Show the stages of cell growth
   B. Observe budding in a plant cell
   C. Predict the genotypes and phenotypes of a particular cross
   D. Create a pattern from population data

10. Genetic Variation passed on to the offspring is caused by which of the following?

    A. Mitosis
    B. Somatic mutations
    C. Germ-line mutations
    D. Translation

11. Yellow fever is a viral disease that is transmitted primarily by mosquitoes.

    An outbreak of yellow fever was reported to have occurred in an area of Africa in February 2020. This outbreak was reported to be spreading to other areas within Africa.

    Which one of the following is a correct statement about this outbreak of yellow fever?

    A. This outbreak of yellow fever is considered to be a pandemic.
    B. Infected individuals who travel to other areas of Africa will not increase the spread of the disease.
    C. This outbreak of yellow fever is occurring in populations with high vaccination rates for yellow fever.
    D. Elimination of mosquito breeding sites in areas with yellow fever will reduce the number of individuals affected.

12. Biotechnologies can be used in the treatment of diabetes. An example is the use of microorganisms to produce the hormone, insulin. This has overtaken the past method of the extraction of insulin from pigs and cattle. What is the main implication of this new method?

A. It is more ethical
B. It is less effective
C. Some vegetarians will object to the use of this new method
D. There will be stricter regulations with labelling.

13. The process below is used to produce transgenic organisms.

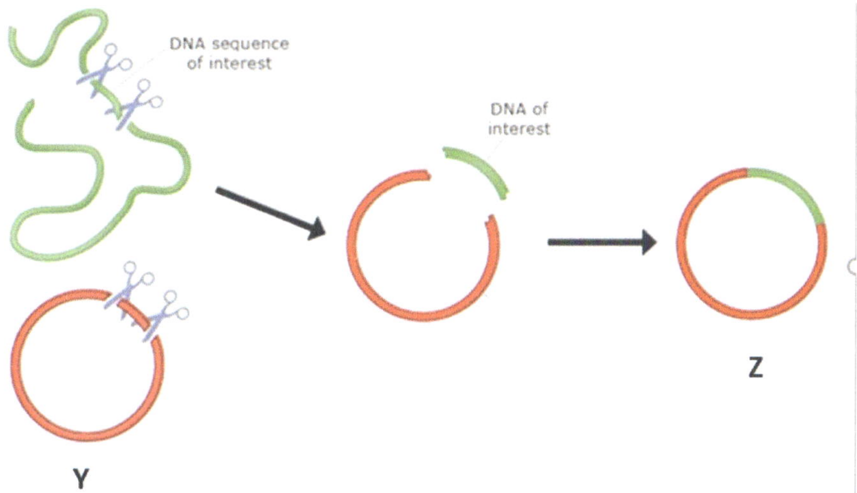

"Y" and "Z" correspond to which of the following?

	Y	Z
A.	Recombinant DNA	Vector
B.	mRNA	Polypeptide Chain
C.	Vector	Recombinant DNA
D.	Restriction Enzymes	Plasmid

14. The diagram below shows the effect of a mutagen on DNA.

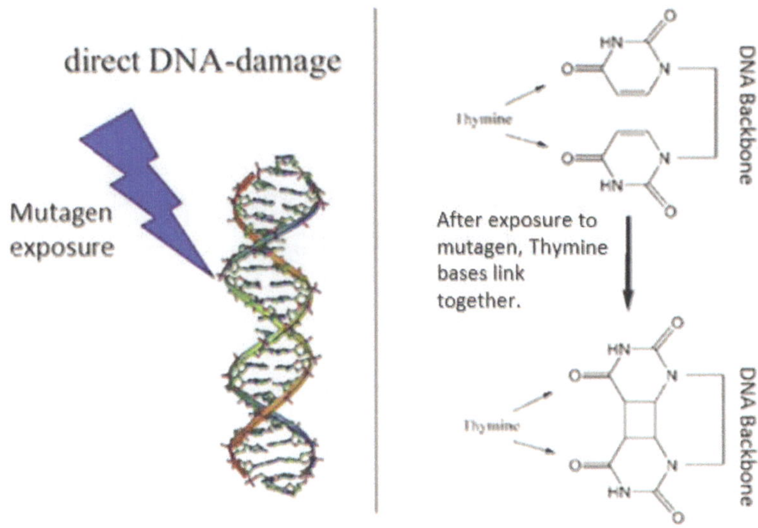

This DNA could be exposed to:

A. A Fungus
B. A Virus
C. A Bacteria
D. Radiation

15. Rabies is a viral disease spread to people by infected animals. A person bitten by an infected animal should be given an injection of specific antibodies.

Following the injection, this person should have

A. Natural active immunity.
B. Artificial active immunity.
C. Natural passive immunity.
D. Artificial passive immunity.

16. To maintain homeostasis many Australian desert mammals, produce relatively dry faeces and concentrated urine.

This type of adaptation would be considered:

A. Behavioural
B. Endothermic
C. Structural
D. Physiological

17. To help maintain blood glucose levels (BGL) at an optimum level in the blood two hormones are involved, glucagon and insulin.

Which of the following statements is correct?

A. When BGL are too high, Beta cells release a hormone called insulin, which causes the body cells to take up glucose
B. When BGL are too low, Beta cells release a hormone called insulin, which causes the body cells to take up glucose.
C. When BGL are too high, Alpha cells release a hormone called glucagon which causes the liver to break down glucose.
D. When BGL are too low, Alpha cells release a hormone called glucagon causing the liver to store sugar as glycogen.

18. Below is a sketch of the human eye a student drew in class, but didn't get time to label it.

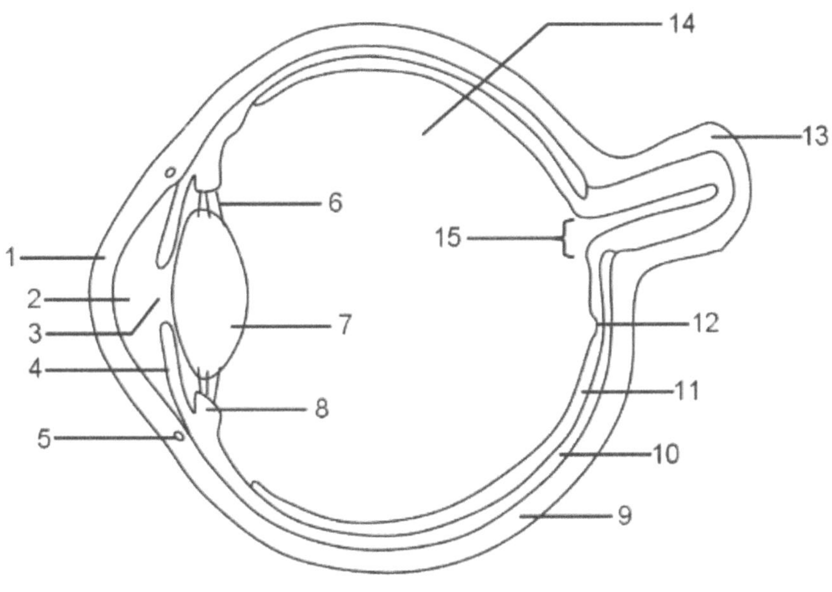

The Human Eye

Structures numbered 1 and 15 are:

A. Sclera and Retina
B. Iris and optic nerve
C. Pupil and Fovea
D. Cornea and Blind Spot

19. The graph below shows the main causes of death worldwide for 2016, based on data from the World Health Organisation. During that year, 56.9 million people died globally.

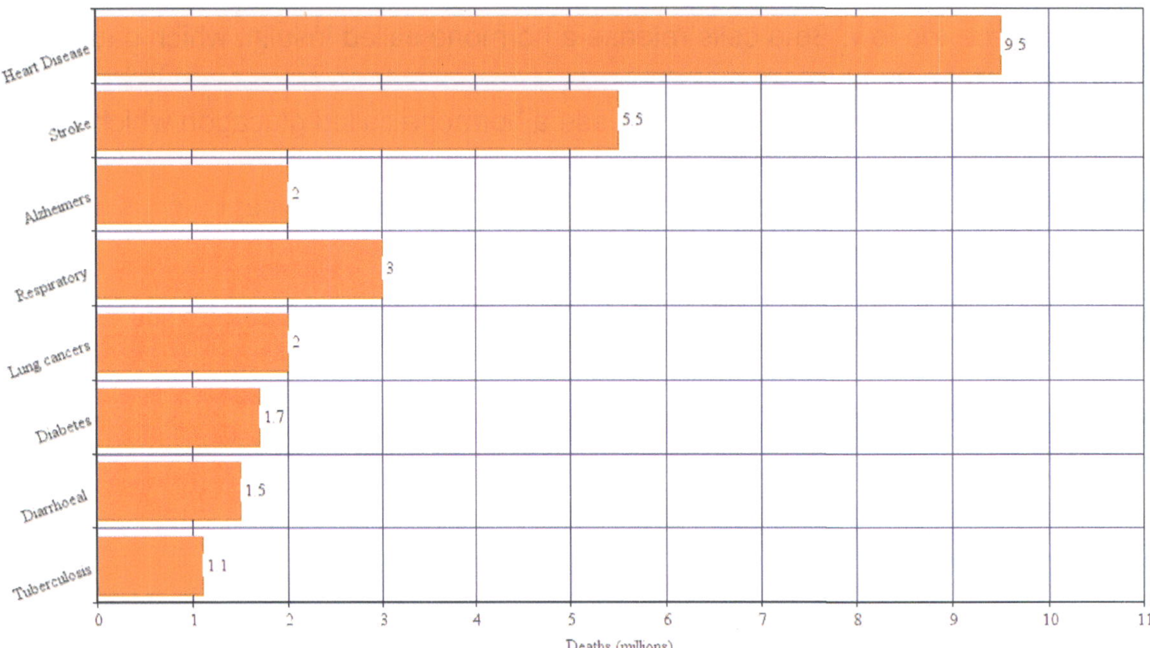

Based on the information presented in the graph you could conclude:

A. Due to modern medicine, less people die from infectious diseases than non-infectious diseases

B. Heart Disease and stroke accounted for approximately 25% of all recorded deaths in 2016.

C. More people die from infectious diseases than non-infectious diseases.

D. Not many people worldwide die from nutritional diseases

20. When comparing kidney dialysis to a normal functioning kidney, which statement is correct?

A. Both remove urea and glucose from the blood but dialysis is more effective as it is a machine

B. A dialysis machine helps maintain homeostasis by reabsorbing salts, glucose and water back into the body

C. A functioning kidney removes urea and also regulates water levels and blood pressure in our body

D. Dialysis is best used 24 hours a day 7 days per week to simulate the functioning of a normal kidney

2021 TRIAL HIGHER SCHOOL CERTIFICATE EXAMINATION

Centre Number

Biology

Section II Answer Booklet

Student Number

80 marks
Attempt Questions 21–35
Allow about 2 hours and 25 minutes for this section

Instructions	• Write your Centre Number and Student Number at the top of this page • Answer the questions in the spaces provided. These spaces provide guidance for the expected length of response. • Show all relevant working in questions involving calculations.

Please turn over

Question 21 (5 marks)

Technological advancement in recombinant DNA technology has enhanced and enriched our knowledge of genetics in the future

(a) Explain how restriction enzymes are used in DNA analysis. 2

....

....

....

....

....

(b) Complete the table by comparing the DNA technological advancements. 3

	Recombinant DNA Technology	**DNA Sequencing**	**DNA profiling**
Structure of DNA			
Used			

Question 22 (4 marks)

The following diagram shows a section from a DNA sequence before and after a mutation.

Normal DNA Sequence

CAC CCC ACT

Mutated DNA Sequence

CAC TCC CAC

(a) What type of mutation is shown in the diagram? 1

....

....

(b) Using the diagram, explain the effect of this type of mutation on the production of a protein. 3

....

....

....

....

....

....

Question 23 (3 marks)

Explain why there are two stages of meiosis and only one stage in mitosis. In your answer, elaborate on the importance that genetic material must be exactly replicated. 3

....

....

Question 24 (4 marks)

Consider the leading causes of death for developing and developed countries:
A student stated that non-infectious diseases cause more deaths than infectious diseases.

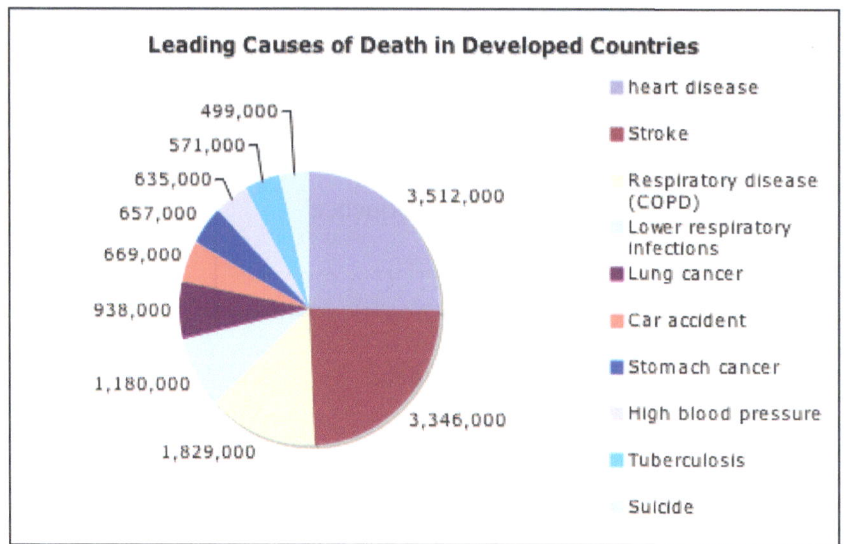

http://www.csun.edu/~sk287035/coursework/646/assignments/data-analysis/2_spreadsheets/7_pie_area.html

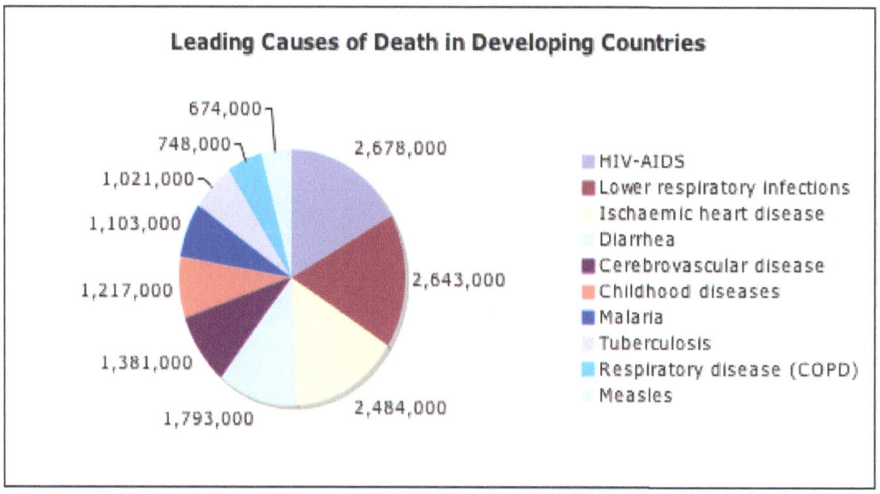

Assess the student's statement using the data shown. 4

....

....

....

....

....

....

....

....

Question 25 (4 marks)

(a) Explain how in cattle a homozygous white animal is crossed with a homozygous red animal to produce offspring that have red and white hair. 3

(b) What is the scientific name given to the offspring from this particular cross? 1

Question 26 (4 marks)

The greater prairie chicken is a small population of a species that lives in three states, Illinois, Kansas and Nebraska. The table shows the changes in the number of alleles and the percentage of eggs hatched during the 1900s.

Location	Population size	Number of alleles per locus	Percentage of eggs hatched
Illinois 1930-1960s 1993	 1,000-25,000 <50	 5.2 3.7	 93 <50
Kansas, 1998	750,000	5.8	99
Nebraska, 1998	75,000 – 200, 000	5.8	96

(a) Compare the data in the table between the state of Illinois and another state. 3

....

....

(b) Outline a possible cause of the change in number of alleles. 1

....

....

Question 27 (5 marks)

(a) Compare the different forms of DNA for prokaryotic and eukaryotic cells. Show this on the Venn diagram. 3

....

....

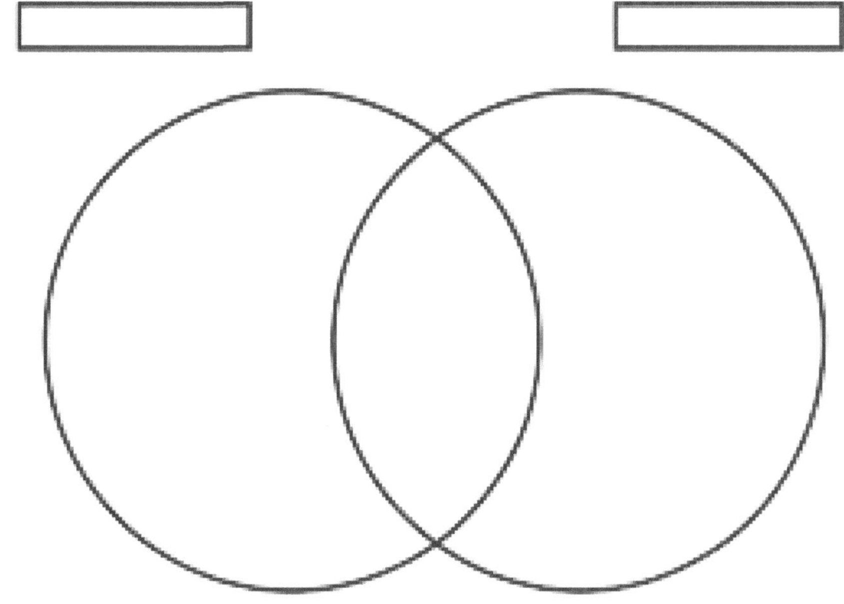

(b) What are non-coding sections of DNA used for in eukaryotic DNA? 2

....

....

Question 28 (5 marks)

(a) Define epidemiology. 1

....

....

(b) Victor noticed that a significant number of students at his school were starting to get sick. They had difficulties breathing, similar to asthma symptoms and were developing lung infections.

This student wondered if the sudden use of "vapes" across the state by young people was causing the students to get sick at his school.

He carried out the following epidemiological study at his school.

Step 1. He surveyed all the students at the school and found out 20% of the students had difficulties breathing or had a lung infection in the last month.

Step 2. He then surveyed all the students at the school and asked how many students have ever vaped? He found out that 20% of the school students at his high school had tried vaping at some stage during the year.

Victor concluded that "**vaping causes breathing difficulties and lung infections**."

Evaluate the method used in Victor's Epidemiological study 4

....

....

....

....

....

....

....

....

....

....

....

....

Question 29 (4 marks)

Explain and evaluate how humans have used developments in selective breeding in animals to improve the future food supply. 4

....
....
....
....
....
....
....
....
....
....
....
....

Question 30 (6 marks)

The genes most commonly affected in hereditary ovaruian cancer are the *BRCA1* and *BRCA2* genes. About 10% of ovarian cancers (about 2,000 women per year) result from inherited mutations in the *BRCA1* and *BRCA2* genes.

Everyone has two copies of the *BRCA1* and *BRCA2* genes, one copy inherited from their mother and one from their father. Even if a person inherits a *BRCA1* or *BRCA2* mutation from one parent, they still have the normal copy of the *BRCA1* or *BRCA2* gene from the other parent. Cancer occurs when a second mutation happens that affects the normal copy of the gene, so that the person no longer has a *BRCA1* or *BRCA2* gene that works properly.

The table below shows the cumulative risk of ovarian cancer depending on the genetic cause.

Age	**Cumulative Risk of Ovarian Cancer %**		
	With BRCA1 mutation	**With BRCA2 mutation**	**No Genetic Cause identified**
30	1.0	0.3	0.1
40	7.0	1.0	0.2
50	21.0	3.0	0.5
60	38.0	19.0	1.0
70	51.0	23.0	3.0
80	64.0	24.0	5.0

(a) Draw an appropriate graph comparing the cumulative risk of ovarian cancer between the BRCA1 mutation and the no genetic cause 4

(b) A doctor has recommended that ovarian cancer screening must be done more frequently after the age of 40, especially for those who have a BRCA1 mutation. Using the graph, justify this recommendation. 2

....

....

....

....

Question 31 (8 marks)

(a) Name a non-infectious disease you have studied in your course. 1

....

(b) Describe a public health program which could help prevent a non-infectious disease. 2

....
....

(c) Evaluate, a genetic technology that could be used to prevent/manage a genetic disease either before birth or after birth 5

....
....
....
....
....
....
....
....
....
....
....
....
....
....
....
....

Question 32 (9 marks)

Staphylococcus aureus (commonly known as staph) are common bacteria. They are usually harmless and many healthy people carry these bacteria on their skin or in their nose. They can be transmitted to another person through contact. Some strains of staph are resistant to the antibiotic called methicillin, and to other antibiotics. These staphs are known as methicillin resistant Staphylococcus aureus (MRSA).

Patients with severe methicillin-resistant Staphylococcus aureus (MRSA) infections are often treated with the IV antibiotic, vancomycin. However, a common side effect of this antibiotic is acute kidney failure requiring temporary dialysis until kidney function is restored.

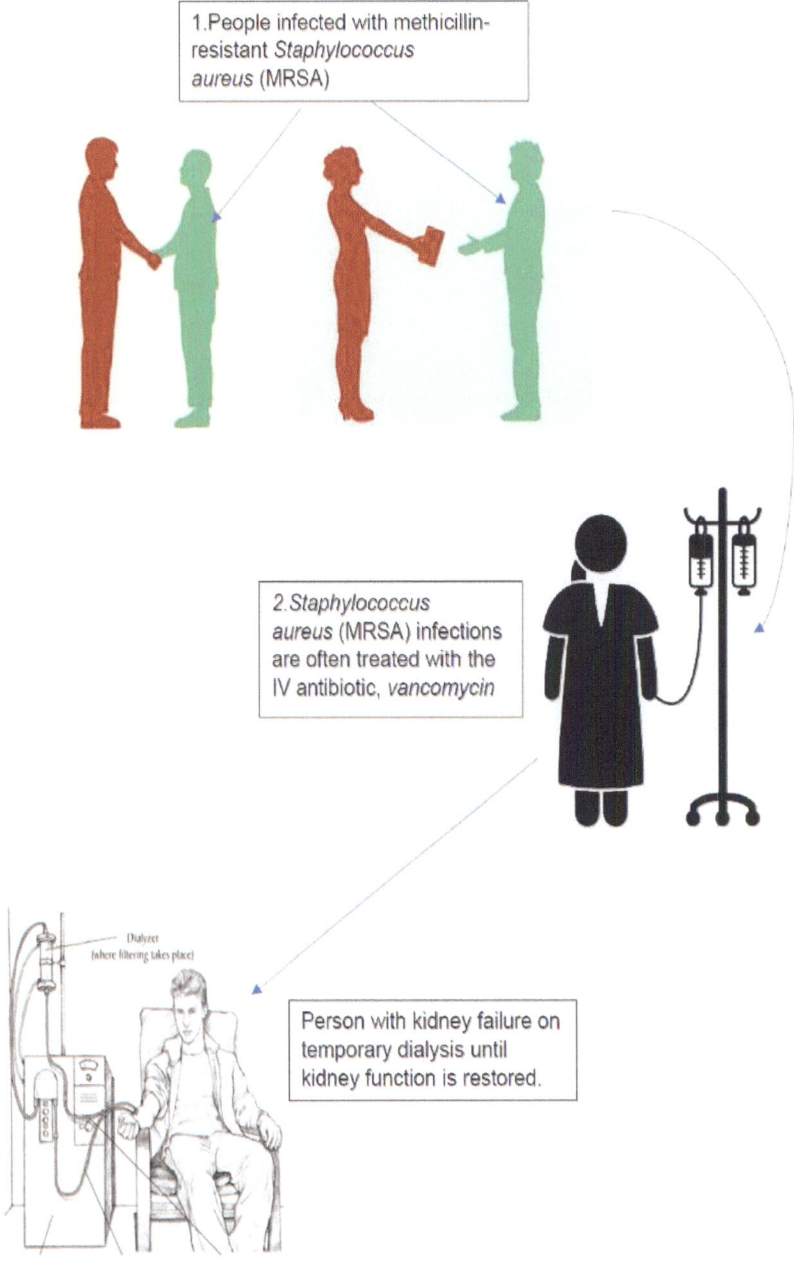

(a) Assess how an understanding of transmission of infectious diseases and antibiotic resistance can reduce the need for kidney transplants due to serious MRSA infection. 6

....
....
....
....
....
....

(b) Explain how dialysis can restore kidney function. 3

....
....
....

Question 33 (3 marks)

The expression of genes can be affected by environmental factors. A student wanted to investigate the effect of light on butterfly wing development and growth. A small group of caterpillars were placed in either green, red or blue light. When the caterpillars developed into butterflies, their wings showed dramatic differences. The findings showed that the caterpillars exposed red light resulted in intensely coloured wings, while exposure to green light resulted in dusky wings. Exposure to blue light led to paler coloured wings.
The student then drew the following conclusion:

"Exposing caterpillars to different colours of light has affected the colour of their developing wings".

Assess the accuracy and validity of this conclusion. 3

....
....
....
....

Question 34 (6 marks)

Below is a diagram that shows the two stages of polypeptide synthesis.

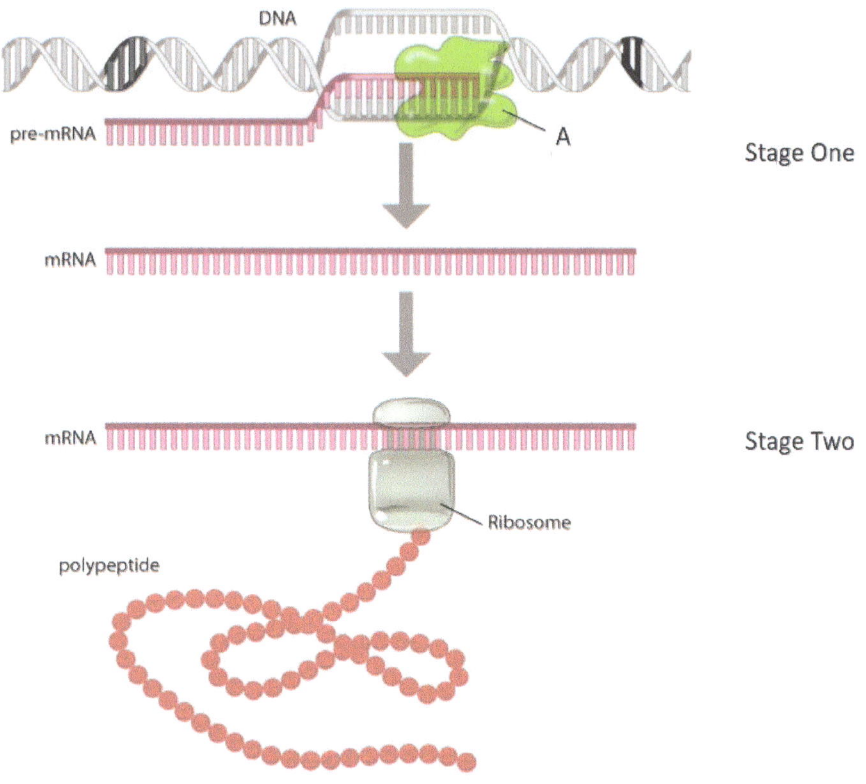

(a) Describe the role of structure "A". 2

....

....

(b) A class of antibiotics called "aminoglycosides" binds to a bacteria's ribosome. This binding site is where the tRNA attaches to. 4

Explain how this binding mechanism disrupts bacterial replication.

....

....

....

....

Question 35 (6 marks)

(a) Define homeostasis. 1

....

....

(b) In the space below construct a flow chart to show how negative feedback occurs in the homeostatic control of body temperature. 5

Marking Guidelines LMC Biology HSC Trial 2021

Section I: Multiple-choice Answer Key

Question	Answer
1	B
2	B
3	A
4	B
5	D
6	A
7	A
8	A
9	C
10	C
11	D
12	A
13	C
14	D
15	D
16	D
17	A
18	D
19	B
20	C

Section II

Question 21 (a)

Criteria	Marks
• Define restrictive enzymes • Explain their use	2
• Define restrictive enzymes	1

Sample answer:
Restrictive enzymes are enzymes that cut DNA at specific sites or sequences. These ends can then be joined to other DNA molecules.

Question 21 (b)

Criteria	Marks
• All 6 correct entries are in the table	3
• 4-5 correct entries are in the table	2
• 2-3 correct entries are in the table	1

(Each entry is worth ½ mark.)

Sample answer:

	Recombinant DNA Technology	**DNA Sequencing**	**DNA profiling**
Structure of DNA	Many copies made from small sample	Exact order of nucleotides on DNA molecule	Microsatellite DNA (Short tandem repeats)
Used	Analyse genome from many organisms	Scientific research such as Human Genome project	Determine identity of individual

Question 22 (a)

Criteria	Marks
• Correctly identifies diagram as a frameshift mutation	1

Sample answer:
Frameshift mutation

Question 22 (b)

Criteria	Marks
• Student refers to the diagram to explain how the insertion changes the amino acid sequence/ reading frame and effects on protein/biochemical processes.	3
• Student refers to diagram to outline that the insertion changes the amino acid sequence/ reading frame **OR**, • Student explains that the insertion results in a non-function protein/affects biochemical processes	2
• Provides some relevant information	1

Sample answer:
A frameshift mutation results in large scale changes to the protein being produced

Question 23

Criteria	Marks
• Explains that there are two stages in Meiosis and one stage in mitosis • States that in Meiosis,the chromosome number is halved whereas the number is the same • In meiosis gametes that allow for variation in a species whereas in mitosis the cloned cells are used in growth and repair. 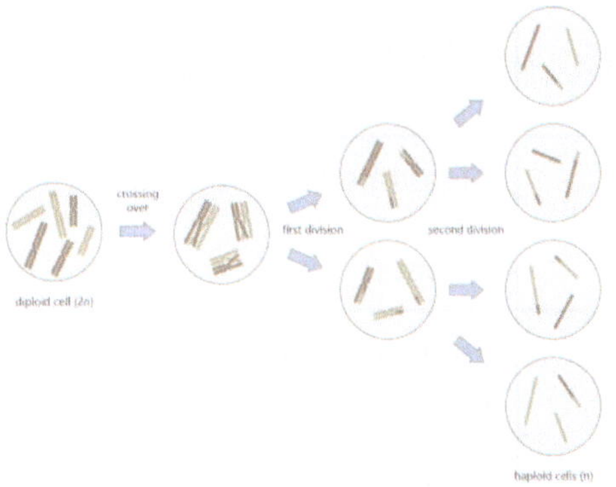 • Explain why there are two stages of meiosis and only one stage in mitosis. In your answer, elaborate on the importance that genetic material must be exactly replicated.	3
• Explains that meiosis produces daughter cells that have a haploid number of chromosomes whereas daughter cells produced in mitosis have the same number as the parent cell	2
• Explains that meiosis produces gametes whereas mitosis produces body cells	1

Question 23 *Sample answer:*
In Meiosis there are two stages so that the chromosome number can be halved (haploid). This allows for variation to occur in the next generation whereas in mitosis, the cells need to be clones of the original as they are used for growth and repair.

Mitosis produces body cells that are exactly copies of the parent cell, diploid number (2N) chromosomes whereas meiosis produces sex cells that have half the number of chromosomes (N) compared to the parent cell

Question 24

Criteria	Marks
• Compares non-infectious to infectious data in developing countries • Compares non-infectious to infectious data in developed countries • Draws valid conclusion on comparison between non-infectious to infectious data worldwide • Uses the data to provide justification for the validity of the conclusion	4
• Compares non-infectious to infectious data • Draws valid conclusion on comparison between non-infectious to infectious data worldwide • Uses the data to provide justification for the validity of the conclusion	3
• Compares non-infectious to infectious data in developing countries • Compares non-infectious to infectious data in developed countries	2
• Compares non-infectious to infectious data	1

Sample answer:

Of the top 10 causes of death worldwide only TWO were due to infectious diseases (around 4 million), while 7 appear to be non-infectious (around 39 million). However, when the data is presented by country status, it is clear that there is a dichotomy. In developing countries, 7 of the top 10 causes of death were infectious diseases (around 11 million) and three were non-infectious diseases (around 4.6 million).

In developed countries, 2 of the top 10 causes of death were infectious (around 1.8 million) while 6 were non-infectious diseases (around 11million). It could be concluded that non-infectious diseases cause more deaths than infectious disease in developed countries, and worldwide, but not in developing countries. However, the data is not complete: there is no indication of the total number of deaths overall, and hence it is not possible to know the effect that causes. It is not possible to determine the truth of the student's statement based on the data provided.

Question 25 (a)

Criteria	Marks
• Uses a punnet square to show homozygous cross • Shows the resulting codominance F1 generation • States that codominance occurs	3
• Explains that a heterozygous cross can result in an offspring with codominance traits	2
• States that the offspring is different to the parents	1

Sample answer:

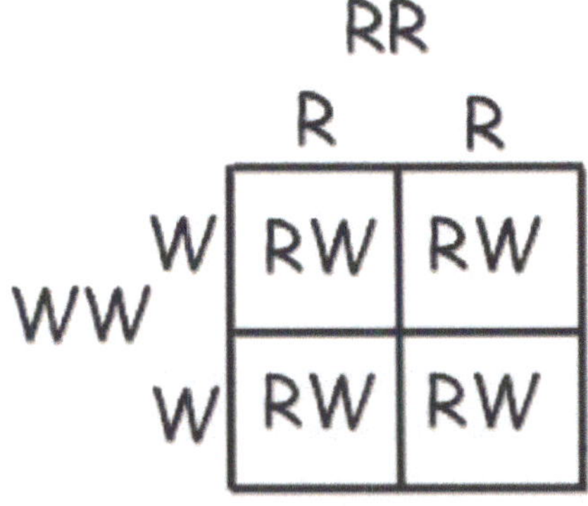

Both alleles expressed in the F1 generation. This is termed codominance where both alleles, red and white are expressed in the offspring. This is a form of incomplete dominance.

Question 25 (b)

Criteria	Marks
• Answer is correct	1

Sample answer:
Roan

Question 26 (a)

Criteria	Marks
• Student refers to the data in the table to compare the change in both the number of alleles and the percentage of eggs hatched in the state of Illinois and another state.	3
• Student refers to the data in the table to compare the change in EITHER the number of alleles or the percentage of eggs hatched in the state of Illinois and another state. Or, • Student compares the change in both the number of alleles and the percentage of eggs hatched in the state of Illinois and another state but does not refer to specific values.	2
• Provides some relevant information	1

Sample answer:
The number of alleles per locus in the state of Illinois during the 1930s is similar to Kansas in 1998, however this number decreased to 3.7 during 1993 in the state of Illinois.

Another change is the percentage of eggs hatched, this number decreased from 93 in 1930s-1960s to less than 50 in the state of Illinois 1993, compared to 99% and 98% in 1998 in Kansas and Nebraska.

Question 26 (b)

Criteria	Marks
•	1

Sample answer:

Question 27 (a)

Criteria	Marks
• Labelled all boxes and Venn diagram correctly • Included at least 3 forms of DNA in both prokaryotic and eukaryotic cells • Correct sides allocated	3
• Labelled all boxes and Venn diagram correctly • Included at least 2 forms of DNA in both prokaryotic and eukaryotic cells • Correct sides allocated	2
• Some of the diagram labelled correctly • Included at least 1 form of DNA in both prokaryotic and eukaryotic cells • Correct sides allocated	1

Sample answer:

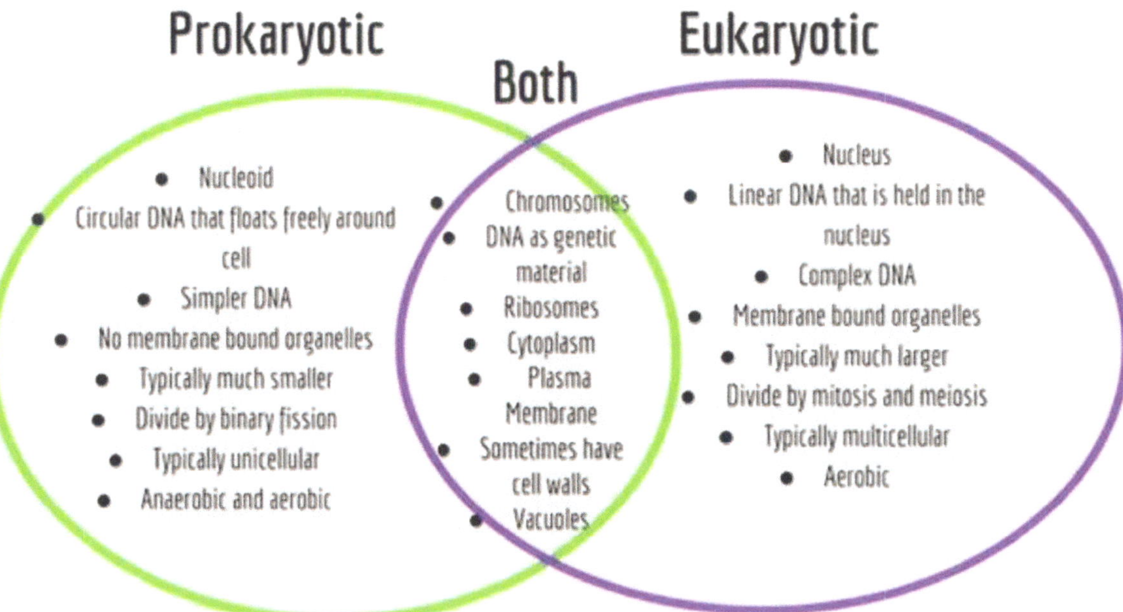

Question 27 (b)

Criteria	Marks
• States that non-coding sections are found in eukaryotic DNA • Used in regulation of cellular processes	2
• Used in a living thing to code for a function	1

Sample answer:
The function of non-coding sections of DNA in eukaryotic cells are in the regulation of cellular processes

Question 28 (a)

Criteria	Marks
• Defines Epidemiology	1

Sample answer:
Epidemiology involves studying the distribution of specific diseases and patterns amongst the people affected. Epidemiology seeks to determine the cause of disease or outbreaks so methods can be developed to control the spread.

Question 28 (b)

Criteria	Marks
• Makes a judgement as to why the conclusion is not valid • Supports the judgement by 3-4 pieces of information which would need to be included to conduct a valid epidemiological study. Including the link between those who vape and those who have breathing problems	4
• Makes a judgement as to why the conclusion is not valid • Supports the judgement by 2-3 pieces of information which would need to be included to conduct a valid epidemiological study.	3
• Makes a judgement as to why the conclusion is not valid • Supports the judgement with some information which would need to be included to conduct a valid epidemiological study.	2
• Provides some relevant information linked to the question and epidemiological studies	1

Sample answer:
Victor's method is not valid. To reach a valid conclusion Victor needed to gather a lot more data to establish cause and effect relationships (that vapes are responsible for the students with breathing difficulties)
He needed to collect data on-

- The number of people without symptoms who vaped /didn't vape
- The number of people with symptoms who vaped/ didn't vape

And compare this data to establish a link.

He also needs to consider other factors which might be responsible , where the students live, their home environments, health history, are they exposed to other pollutants in their environment, family history of breathing difficulties, students diets,

A far more extensive collation of data is needed before a cause and effect relationship could be established.

Question 29

Criteria	Marks
• Explains that manipulation of animal reproduction occurs in agriculture • Evaluates how and why humans breed the best animals for consumption that require less time to grow and are less prone to disease or are disease free • States that there is an increasing world population and that demand for food is increasing. • Lists at least 3 selective breeding techniques (such as artificial insemination, embryo transfer techniques, storage of favourable gametes for later use and genetic engineering)	4
• Explains that manipulation of animal reproduction occurs in agriculture • Evaluates how humans breed the best animals for consumption • States that there is an increasing world population and that demand for food is increasing. • Lists at least 2 selective breeding techniques (such as artificial insemination, embryo transfer techniques, storage of favourable gametes for later use and genetic engineering)	3
• States that manipulation of animal reproduction occurs in agriculture • States that there is an increasing world population and that demand for food is increasing. • Lists at least 1 selective breeding technique (such as artificial insemination, embryo transfer techniques, storage of favourable gametes for later use and genetic engineering)	2
• States that manipulation of animal reproduction occurs and that humans selectively breed animals for consumption	1

Sample answer:
With an increasing world population, demand for food is increasing. Humans use of selective breeding techniques such as artificial insemination, embryo transfer techniques, storage of favourable gametes for later use and genetic engineering, has allowed for the breeding of the best animals for consumption that require less time to grow and are less prone to disease or are disease free.

Question 30 (a)

Criteria	Marks
• Appropriate graph drawn using data points of BRCA1 mutation and the no genetic cause column. Student differentiates between the two data sets using a key or any other type of labelling	4
• Appropriate graph drawn using data points of BRCA1 mutation and the no genetic cause column. No differentiation between the two data sets using a key or any other type of labelling.	3
• An appropriate graph showing one data set is drawn, **OR** • Incorrect type of graph is drawn using both data sets.	2
• Attempts to draw a graph.	1

Sample answer:

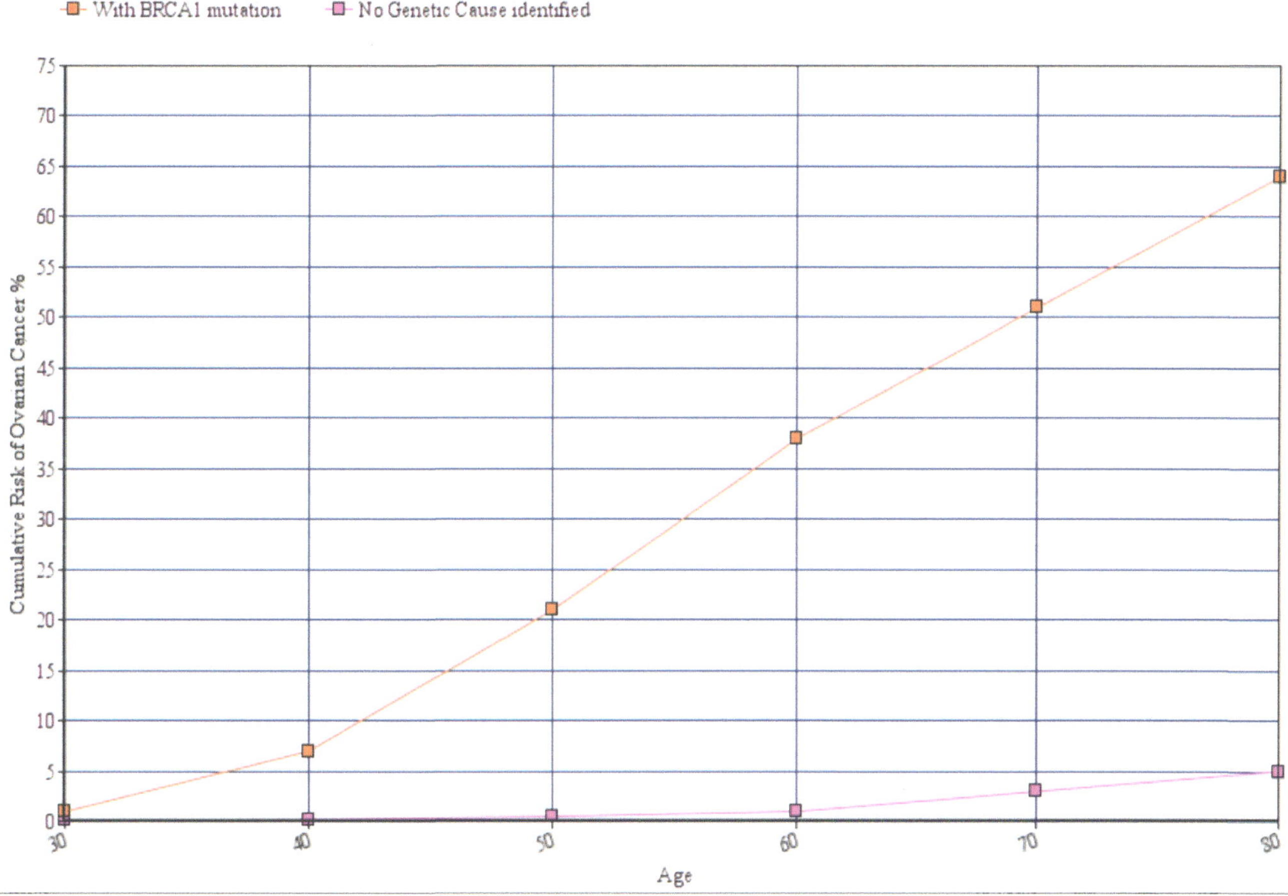

Question 30 (b)

Criteria	Marks
• Justifies the recommendation by referring to the data and the trend from the graph.	2
• Identifies the trend from the graph **OR,** • Provides any other relevant information from the graph	1

Sample answer:
From the age of 40, we can see a tri-fold increase in the % cumulative risk of developing ovarian cancer for those with the BRCA1 mutation and this increase continues with age.

Question 31 (a)

Criteria	Marks
• Names a non-infectious disease	1

Sample answer:
Lung cancer

Question 31 (b)

Criteria	Marks
• Describes an example of a program and links it to how it has helped prevent a named Non-infectious disease	2
• Names a program and links it to a non-infectious disease	1

Sample answer:
Public health campaigns have been very effective in reducing the number of people who smoke in Australia and hence a decrease in the number of people with smoking related lung cancer.
TV advertisements warning of the dangers of smoking combined with a ban on advertising cigarettes (plain packaging also), and restrictions as to where in public you can smoke have greatly reduced the uptake of smoking in Australia.

Question 31 (c)

Criteria	Marks
• Describes a genetic technology in detail, and links it to a named disease which it could prevent and / or manage. • Makes a valued judgment about the use of the technology	5
• Describes a genetic technology, and links it to a named disease which it could prevent and / or manage. • Makes a valued judgment about the use of the technology	4
• Names a genetic technology, and links it to a named disease which it could prevent and / or manage. • Makes a valued judgment about the use of the technology	3
• Names a genetic technology and links it to a disease it can prevent/control	2
• Names a genetic technology	1

Sample answer:
Cystic Fibrosis is an autosomal recessive condition whereby those affected have a reduced life span due to a build-up of fluid on their lungs.
If both parents carry the recessive allele then there is a 25% chance that they will have a child with CF. Left unchecked, parents only know if they both carry the allele if they conceive a CF child.

The genes responsible for CF have been identified so pre-implantation genetic screening is a technology that can be used in IVF patients to determine if the embryo carries the gene. If so the embryo is not implanted.

In practice this can prevent offspring inheriting this disease.

A sample of cells Biopsy) is taken from an embryo at day 5.
After removing the embryonic cells in the biopsy, scientists transfer the sample to a small test tube. A technique called Whole Genome Amplification is used to make millions of copies of the embryonic DNA.

This DNA is then fragmented (broken up), and hundreds of thousands of these small embryonic DNA fragments are sequenced (analysed) at the same time. Specialised software is used to compare each fragment against the human genome - the standard map of human genes. From here, abnormalities in genes and chromosomes can be identified.

This technology has the potential to remove many of the common genetic diseases in humans but there are ethical considerations also. Many religious groups and society in general have issues with screening 5 day old embryos, potentially discarding those with genetic abnormalities. Who has the right to make the judgement as to what is genetically "normal"?

Question 32 (a)

Criteria	Marks
• Identifies direct transmission using the information/diagram provided and links their understanding to transmission of infectious diseases • Has an extensive understanding of the serious nature of antibiotic resistance and can deduce the need for kidney transplants due to serious MRSA infection.	6
• Identifies direct transmission using the information/diagram provided and has an understanding of transmission of infectious diseases and antibiotic resistance. • Can deduce that this can result in kidney failure due to serious MRSA infection.	5
• Identifies transmission can occur and uses the information provided and on infectious diseases and antibiotic resistance and links them to the need for kidney transplants as a result of the infection.	4
• Identifies transmission using the information/diagram provided and has an understanding of antibiotic resistance. • Also understands that kidney failure requires a kidney transplant.	3
• Uses the information/diagram provided and has basic knowledge regarding the transmission of infectious diseases. • Has basic knowledge about antibiotic resistance and the need for kidney transplants due to serious MRSA infection.	2
• Has a limited knowledge of infectious disease and its transmission. Mentions antibiotic resistance and the need for kidney transplants	1

Sample answer:
Staphylococcus aureus (commonly known as staph) are common bacteria. They are usually harmless and many healthy people carry these bacteria on their skin or in their nose. They can be transmitted to another person through contact. Some strains of staph are resistant to the antibiotic called methicillin, and to other antibiotics. These staph are known as methicillin resistant Staphylococcus aureus (MRSA).

Patients with severe *methicillin-resistant Staphylococcus aureus* (MRSA) infections are often treated with the IV antibiotic, ***vancomycin***. However a common side effect of this antibiotic is acute kidney failure requiring temporary dialysis until kidney function is restored.

Question 32 (b)

Criteria	Marks
• Explains that dialysis maintains water balance in the body, keeping the nutrients, wastes and chemicals at a safe level	3
• Briefly explains dialysis and that it helps keep the body at a safe level	2
• Provides a basic understanding of dialysis and its function	1

Sample answer:
Dialysis keeps your body in balance by removing waste, salt and extra water to prevent them from building up in the body. Dialysis also keeps the level of certain chemicals in your blood, such as potassium, sodium and bicarbonate at safe levels and this helps control blood pressure.

Question 33

Criteria	Marks
• Makes a judgment about the conclusion by referring to there being no control group and a small sample size.	3
• Makes a judgment about the conclusion by EITHER referring to - there being no control group, **OR,** - a small sample size.	2
• Any relevant information about the validity or accuracy of the method is provided.	1

Sample answer:
The conclusion is not accurate as the student only sampled a small population size and since there was no control group, that is, caterpillars not exposed to any light, this makes the conclusion not valid.

Question 34 (a)

Criteria	Marks
• Student identifies that structure A is RNA polymerase and outlines the function of this enzyme.	2
• Student identifies that structure A is RNA polymerase, **OR** • Outlines the role without identifying what structure A is.	1

Sample answer:

Question 34 (b)

Criteria	Marks
• Student describes the process of translation and explains the effect of the antibiotic on the process and correctly links this disruption to the inhibition of the growth/survival of the bacterial cell.	4
• Student describes the process of translation and explains the effect of the antibiotic on the process, however does not link this disruption to the inhibition of the growth/survival of the bacterial cell. **OR** • Student describes the process of translation and outlines the effect of the antibiotic on the process, and links this disruption to the inhibition of the growth/survival of the bacterial cell.	3
• Student describes the process of translation **OR** • Identifies the effect of the antibiotic on the process and links this to the growth/survival of the bacteria.	2
• Any relevant information is provided.	1

Sample answer:
During stage 2, the mRNA strand must combine with the tRNA on the ribosome site so that the anticodons on the tRNA molecule match the codons from mRNA strand, resulting in the formation of polypeptide bonds between amino acids. This polypeptide chain is necessary for the formation of a protein that has an important role in the growth/survival of the bacteria. The binding of the aminoglycoside to the ribosome will prevent this, resulting in no polypeptide chain formed. This inhibits the growth of the bacteria.

Question 35 (a)

Criteria	Marks
• Correct definition of Homeostasis	1

Sample answer:
The maintenance of a relative stable internal environment, eg Human body temp 36.5°C

Question 35 (b)

Criteria	Marks
• Draws a flow chart indicating optimal temperature, temp rise above and below optimal, how it is detected, response of effectors and return to optimum temp. Arrows indicating direction of flow chart.	5
• Draws a flow chart indicating optimal temperature, temp rise above and below optimal, how it is detected, response of effectors and return to optimum temp.	4
• Draws parts of a flow chart indicating optimal temperature, temp rise above OR below optimal, how it is detected, response of effectors and return to optimum temp **OR** • Draws a flow chart indicating optimal temperature, temp rise above and below optimal, t is detected (in general terms), response of effectors..	3
• Indicates a response when temp increases and when temp decreases.	2
• Names a response when temp rises or falls.	1

Sample answer:

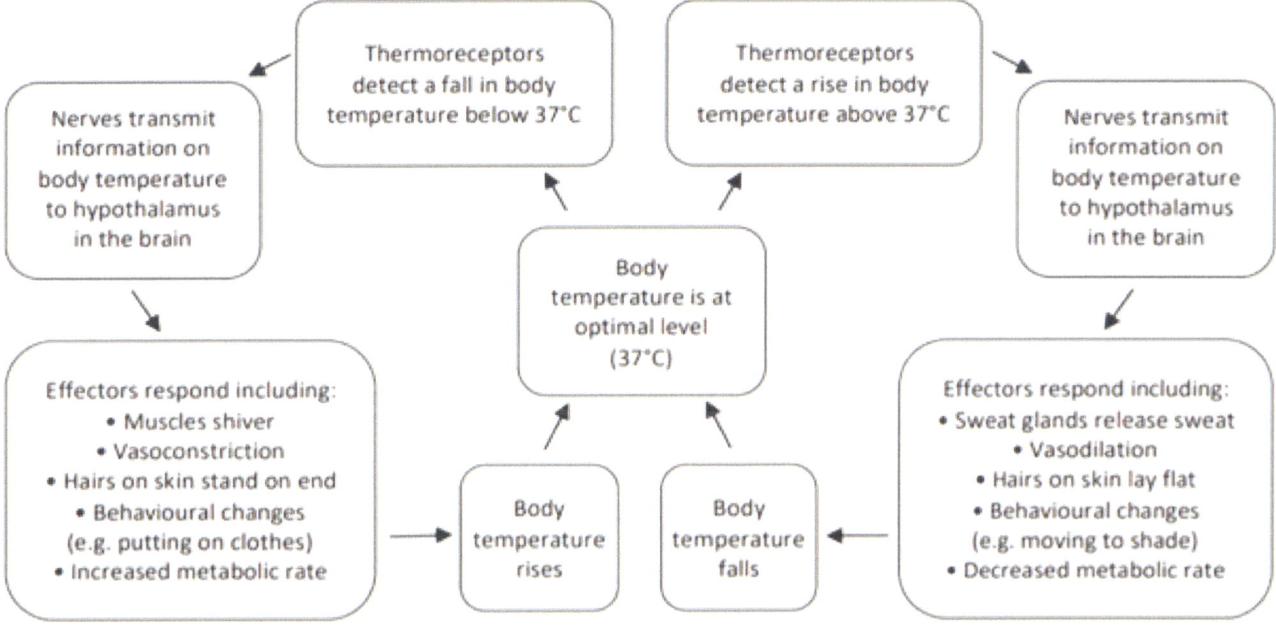

Mapping Grid

Section I

Q	Marks	Content	Syllabus Outcomes
1	1	Reproduction	(5.1.1)
2	1	Reproduction	(5.1.1)
3	1	Reproduction	(5.1.2)
4	1	Cell replication	(5.2.1)
5	1	Causes of Infectious Disease	(7.1.1)
6	1	Prevention, Treatment and Control	(7.3.2)
7	1	DNA and Polypeptide Synthesis	(5.3.3)
8	1	Genetic Variation	(5.4.2)
9	1	Mutation	(6.1.5)
10	1	Prevention, Treatment and Control	(7.4.4)
11	1	Biotechnology	(6.2.1)
12	1	Biotechnology	(6.3.4)
13	1	Mutation	(6.1.1)
14	1	Immunity	(7.3.1)
15	1	Homeostasis	(8.1.2)
16	1	Homeostasis	(8.1.2)
17	1	Homeostasis	(8.1.1)
18	1	Technology and Disorders	(8.5.1)
19	1	Causes and Effects	(8.2.1)
20	1	Technology and Disorders	(8.5.2)

Section II

Q	Marks	Content	Syllabus Outcomes
21	6	Inheritance Patterns in a Population	(5.5.1)
22	4	Mutation	(6.1.2)
23	3	Mutation	(6.1.2)
24	7	Cause and Effect	(8.2.1)
25	4	Genetic Variation	(5.4.2)
26	4	Mutation	(6.1.6)
27	5	DNA and Polypeptide Synthesis	(5.3.1)
28	5	Epidemiology	(8.3.1)
29	4	Reproduction	(5.1.3)
30	6	Inheritance Patterns in a population	(5.5.2)
31	8	Prevention	(8.4.1)
32	9	Technologies and Disorders	(8.5.2)
33	3	DNA and Polypeptide Synthesis	(5.3.2)
34	6	DNA and Polypeptide Synthesis	(5.3.2)
35	6	Homeostasis	(8.5.1)

2022 YEAR 11 EXAMINATION	
BIOLOGY	
General Instructions	• Reading time – 5 minutes • Working time – 2 hours • Write using black pen • Draw diagrams using pencil • Calculators approved by NESA may be used
Total marks: 75	Section I – 20 marks (pages 2–10) • Attempt Questions 1–20 • Allow about 35 minutes for this section
	Section II – 55 marks (pages 12–21) • Attempt Questions 21–28 • Allow about 1 hours and 25 minutes for this section

Section I

20 marks
Attempt Questions 1–20
Allow about 35 minutes for this section

Use the multiple-choice answer sheet for Questions 1–20.

1. What is an autotroph?

   A. an organism capable of producing its own nutritional substances
   B. an organism unable to create its own nutritional substances
   C. an organism that breaks organic substances into inorganic substances
   D. an organism that breaks inorganic substances into organic substances

2. Which organelle is responsible for cellular respiration in a eukaryotic cell?

   A. Cytoplasm
   B. Ribosome
   C. Mitochondria
   D. Vacuole

3. Stains and dyes are used to help view cellular structures under the light microscope.

   The advantage of stains and dyes in microscopy is to:

   A. Make the cells attractive to view
   B. To magnify the specimen being viewed
   C. Highlight structures being viewed
   D. Clean the specimen before mounting on a slide

4. Increasing the abundance of predators in an area for a particular species is most likely to:

   A. Increase the abundance of the particular species
   B. Increase the distribution of the particular species
   C. Act as a positive selection pressure
   D. Act as a negative selection pressure

5. Dolphins are mammals and sharks are fish, but both have streamlined bodies to help them move through the water quickly. This is an example of:

   A. Convergent evolution
   B. Divergent evolution
   C. Punctuated equilibrium
   D. Parallel evolution

6. Which term best describes corals?

   A. unicellular
   B. colonial
   C. multicellular
   D. eukaryotes

7. Darwin's Finches are an example of speciation through evolution. In this case, the speciation is thought to have been originally caused by:

   A. Geographical isolation
   B. Predators
   C. Reproductive isolation
   D. Climate change

8. Which of the following adaptations could be found in a plant surviving in a high salt environment?

   A. Absorbing and storing salt in the roots only
   B. Actively secreting salt through glands on the leaves
   C. Decreasing water intake
   D. Decreased size and number of vacuoles

9. A melting glacier exposed the remains of a woolly mammoth. Which method would be most appropriate to date the age of it?

   A. ice core samples
   B. gas analysis
   C. radiocarbon dating
   D. uranium dating

10. A student varied the substrate concentration during an enzyme activity experiment. He graphed the results and observed that increasing the substrate concentration had no effect on the enzyme rate of reaction.

    What does the 'X' on the line represent?

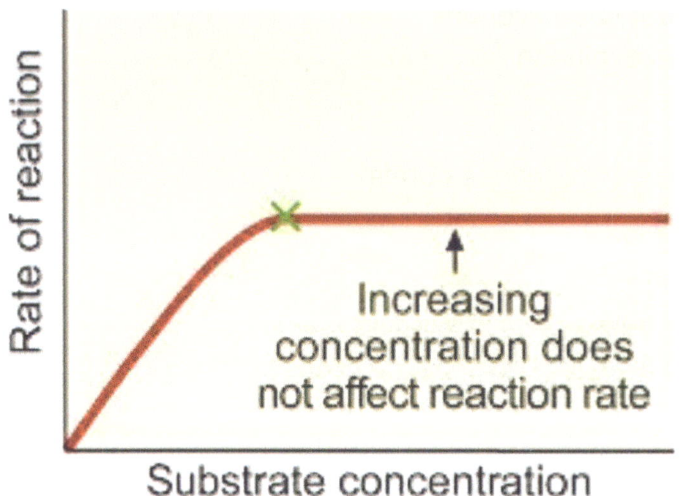

    A. Enzyme concentration
    B. Point of saturation
    C. Enzyme set point
    D. Value of the reaction rate

11.

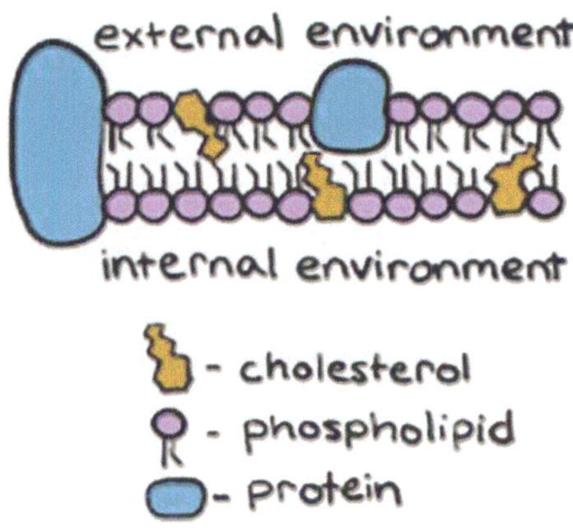

    Modelling in Biology is a useful tool. What does the image above represent?

    A. Fluid mosaic model
    B. A DNA molecule
    C. Osmosis
    D. Cellular respiration

12. Correctly identify the cells below.

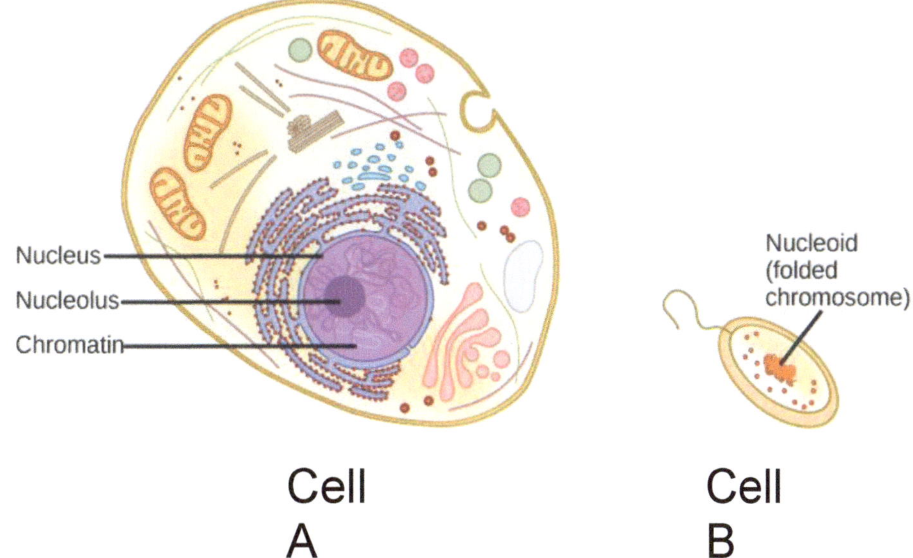

	Cell A	Cell B
A.	Stem Cell	Prokaryote
B.	Eukaryote	Stem Cell
C.	Prokaryote	Eukaryote
D.	Eukaryote	Prokaryote

13. The following diagram compares the developmental stages of different species.

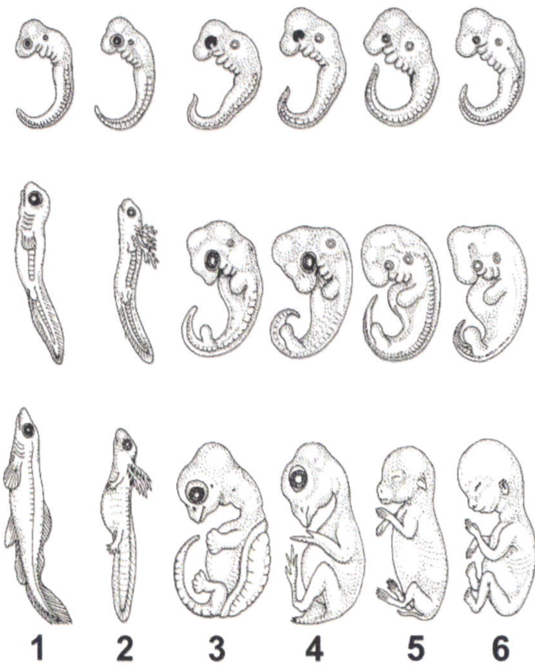

From the diagram, and using the principles of comparative embryology, which two species do you predict are most closely related:

A. 1 & 6
B. 2 & 6
C. 5 & 6
D. 4 & 5

14. The transport system shown in the diagram is:

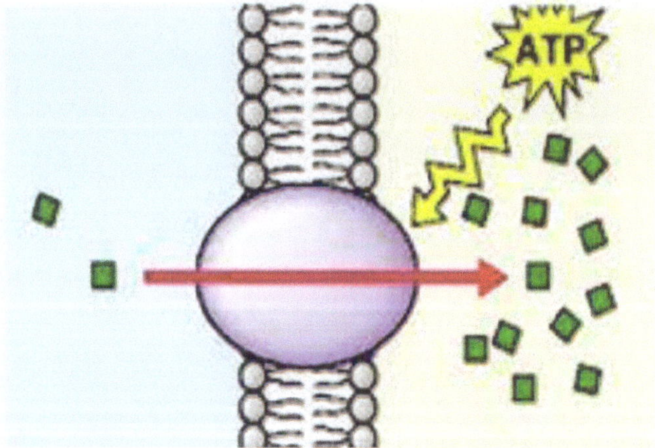

A. Diffusion
B. Active Transport
C. Cytokinesis
D. Transduction

15.

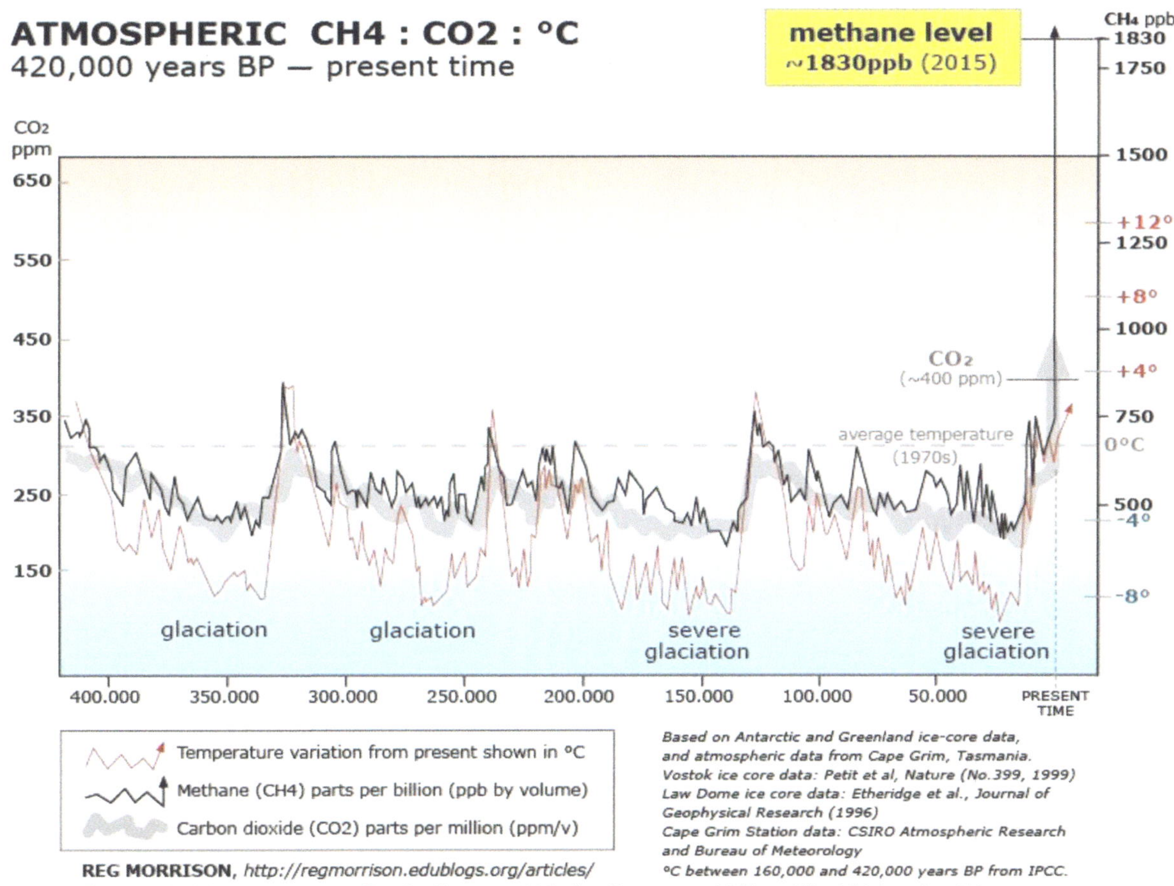

https://upload.wikimedia.org/wikipedia/commons/9/96/Graph_CO2_CH4_and_Temperature_Graph_in_English_15_June_2015_by_Reg_Morrison.jpg

The graph suggests that there was a severe glaciation event that ended just over ten thousand years ago.

Suggest a suitable adaptation for such an event.

A. more sweat glands
B. increased panting
C. reducing the amount of fur or hair on the body
D. increasing the amount of fur or hair on the body

16. The diagram below shows a biological survey done around an aquatic area.

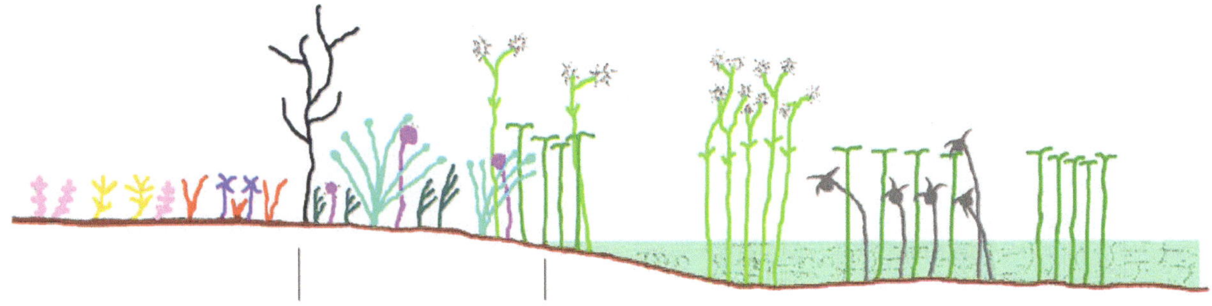

https://upload.wikimedia.org/wikipedia/commons/c/c9/Macta_transect.jpg

The best description of this survey would be:

A. catch and release
B. survey
C. quadrat
D. transect

17. The diagram shows three ways that nutrients can be absorbed into a cell. This is best described as:

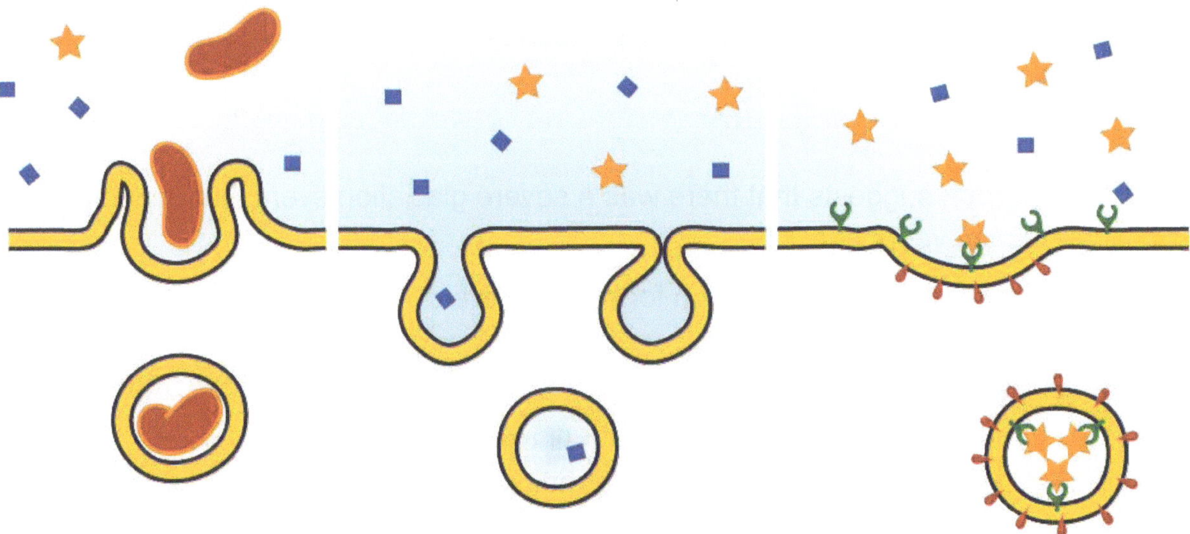

https://upload.wikimedia.org/wikipedia/commons/e/e2/0309_Three_Forms_of_Endocytosis_cleaned.jpg

A. endocytosis
B. exocytosis
C. diffusion
D. osmosis

18. The graph shows some data related to the levels of glucose and insulin in the body.

A pre-diabetic patient needs to follow a diet to allow slower changes in their glucose and insulin levels.

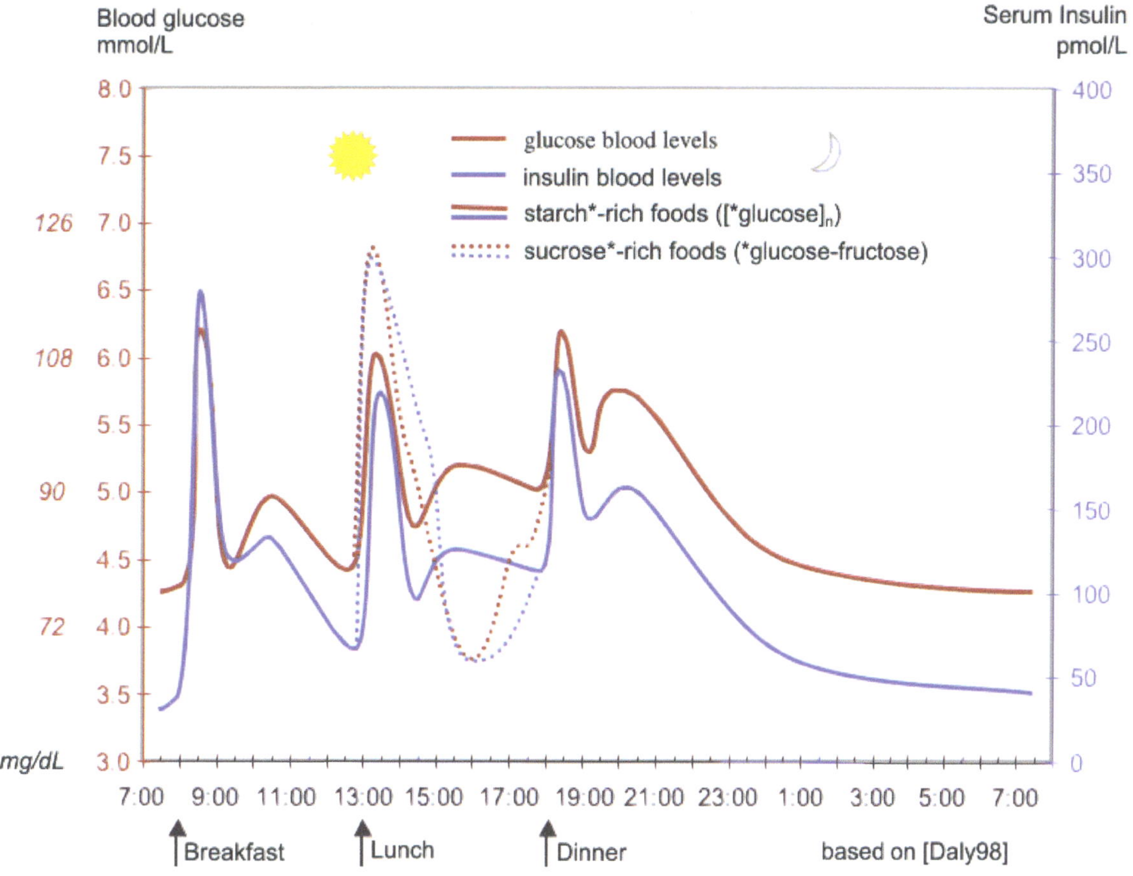

https://upload.wikimedia.org/wikipedia/commons/9/92/Glucose-insulin-day-english.svg

According to the graph they should:

A. only eat after midnight
B. eat nothing at lunch
C. eat sucrose rich food
D. eat starch rich foods

19. The image below shows a clown fish taking shelter in a sea anemone.

This is an example of:

A. predation
B. competition
C. disease
D. symbiosis

20. Which correctly names the vascular systems in plants and animals?

	Plants	**Animals**
A.	arteries and veins	xylem and phloem
B.	xylem and phloem	arteries and veins
C.	arteries and phloem	xylem and veins
D.	xylem and veins	arteries and phloem

2022 PRELIMINARY EXAMINATION	
Biology **Section II Answer Booklet**	Centre Number
	Student Number

55 marks
Attempt Questions 21–28
Allow about 1 hours and 25 minutes for this section

Instructions	• Write your Centre Number and Student Number at the top of this page • Answer the questions in the spaces provided. These spaces provide guidance for the expected length of response. • Show all relevant working in questions involving calculations.

Please turn over

Question 21 (3 marks)

The diagram below shows a cross section of a leaf.

(a) Name and label the structure on the diagram that is involved in gaseous exchange between the plant and the atmosphere. 1

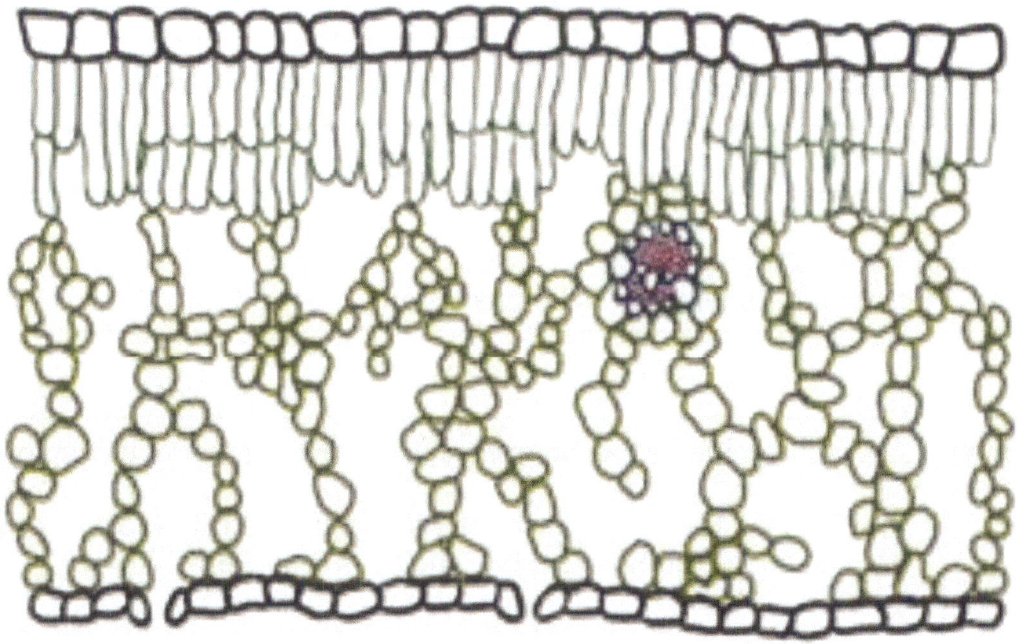

(b) Outline what osmosis is and how it is involved in supplying water for photosynthesis. 2

....

....

....

....

Question 22 (4 marks)

Sclerophyll plants are typically found in climates with mild winters and hot and dry summers.

Describe two adaptations that they use to cope with these conditions.

....

....

....

....

....

....

....

....

Question 23 (6 marks)

The diagram below shows an investigation into digestion.

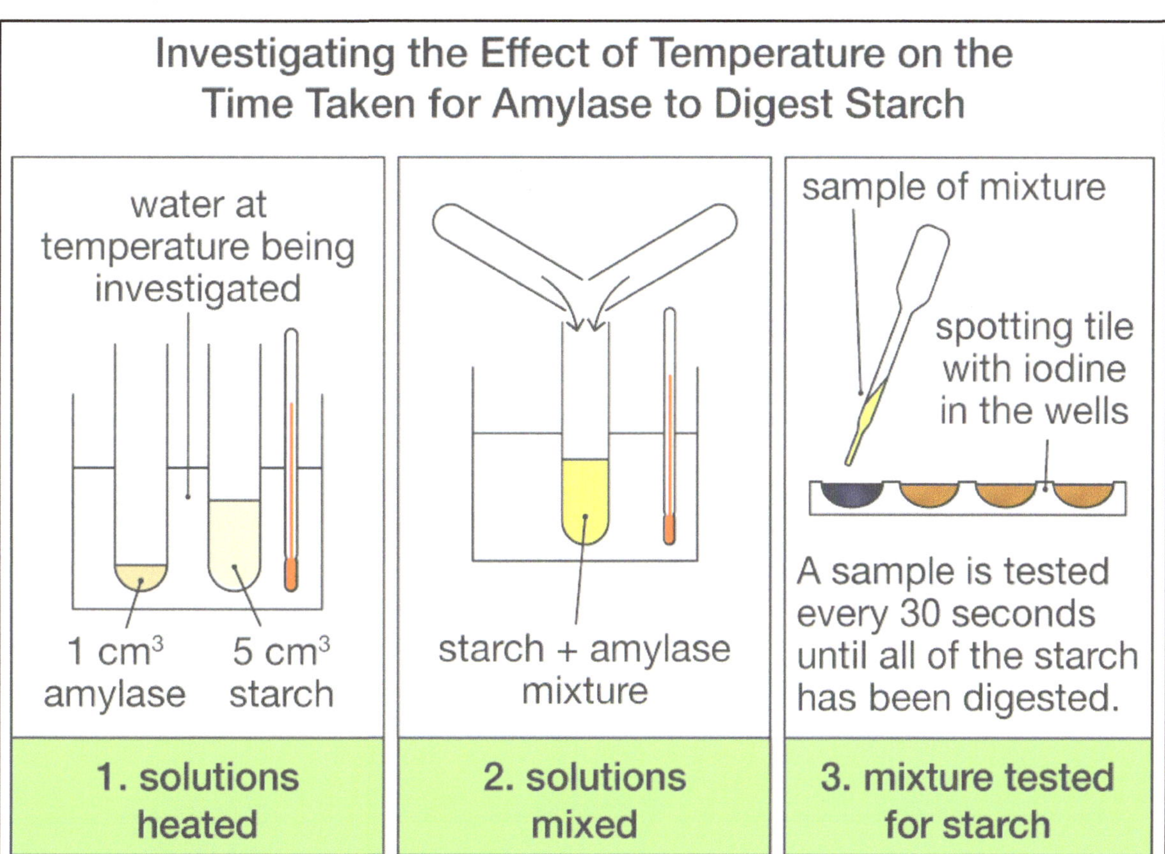

https://www.lbq.org/Search/Biology?quickRef=11676

(a) Explain why the solutions were heated in step 1. 1

....

....

(b) A sample was taken at regular intervals in step 3. Why was this important? 1

....
....

(c) Describe how reliability could be improved in this investigation. 2

....
....
....
....
....
....

(d) Explain how starch is digested by amylase. 2

....
....
....
....

Question 24 (6 marks)

The image below compares two mammalian digestive systems.

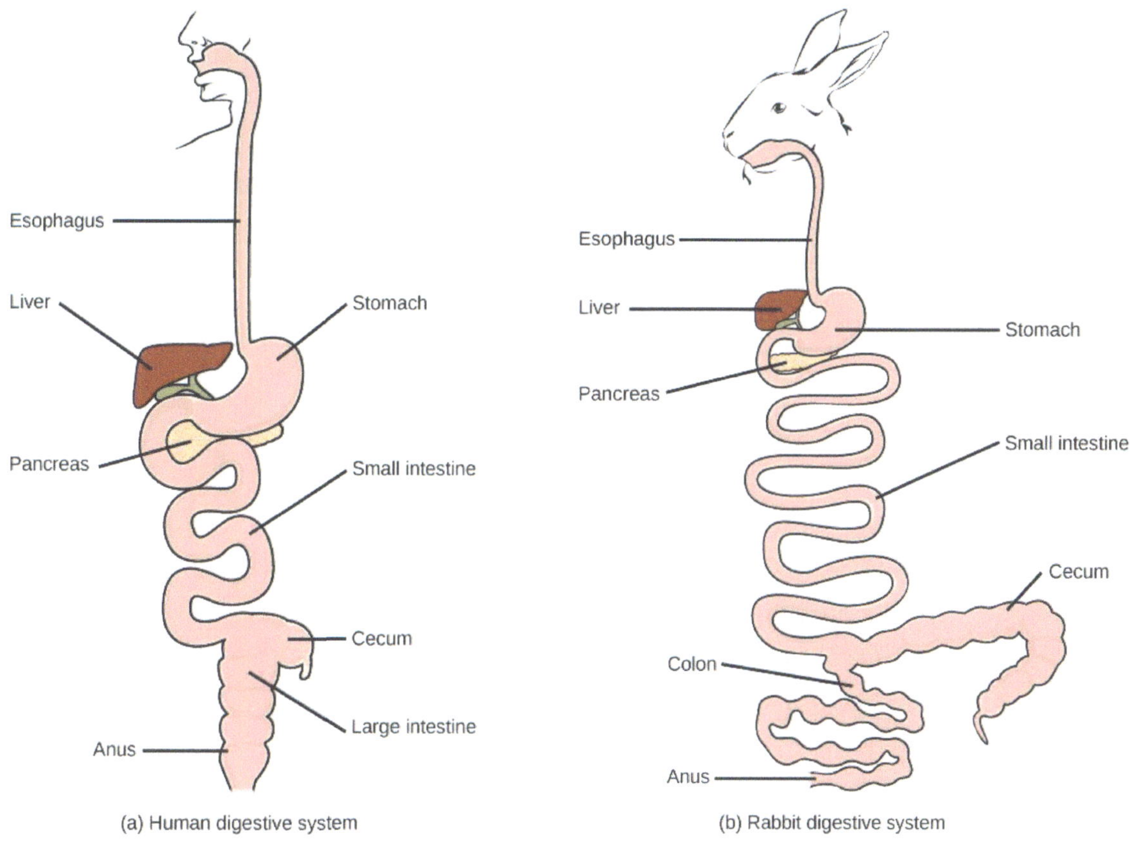

https://upload.wikimedia.org/wikipedia/commons/7/7a/Figure_34_01_05ab.jpg

(a) Explain how one organ in the diagram aids in chemical digestion. 2

....
....
....
....

(b) Both systems utilise the same pathway and organs, however, there is a difference in the size of some of these organs. Explain why in reference to the organ mentioned in part (a). 4

....
....
....
....
....
....

Question 25 (8 marks)

The distribution of the cane toad Rhinella marina has grown since the introduction of the species to Australia in the 1930s. Since the 1980s this pest species has spread further west into the Northern Territory and Western Australia, and further south into New South Wales.

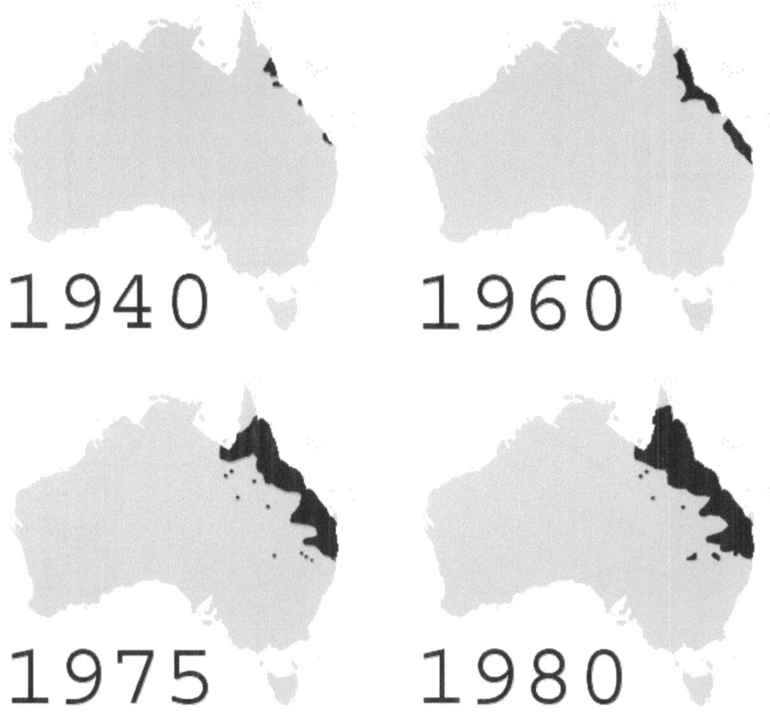

(a) Describe two reasons why the cane toad has been so successful in spreading across many areas of Australia. 4

....
....
....
....
....
....
....
....

(b) Researchers have found that red-bellied black snakes that live in cane toad-infested areas had smaller heads relative to their body sizes, when compared to red-bellied black snakes from areas free of cane toads. 4

With your understanding of selection pressures, explain how the presence of cane toads has affected the evolution of red-bellied black snake populations.

....
....
....
....

Question 26 (6 marks)

(a) Below are examples of adaptations to assist survival. Complete the information for each one. 6

Fat stored in the hump of a camel

Type of adaptation: ....

How this adaptation assists survival: ....

....

....

The platypus builds burrows near the water-edge

Type of adaptation: ....

How this adaptation assists survival: ....

....

....

Plant on the lower canopy of the rainforest has wide, plate-like leaves

Type of adaptation: ....

How this adaptation assists survival: ....

....

....

Question 27 (6 marks)

Enzymes require optimal conditions to work effectively. Briefly explain how enzymes work and use an annotated diagram to describe what happens when conditions are not optimal for them 6

....
....
....
....
....
....

Question 28 (16 marks)

The graph below shows a visualisation of data on coral bleaching in the australiasian region since 1980.

The data in red shows severe bleaching events where more than 30% of the reefs have been affected, while the blue describes events where less than 30% of the reef's were.

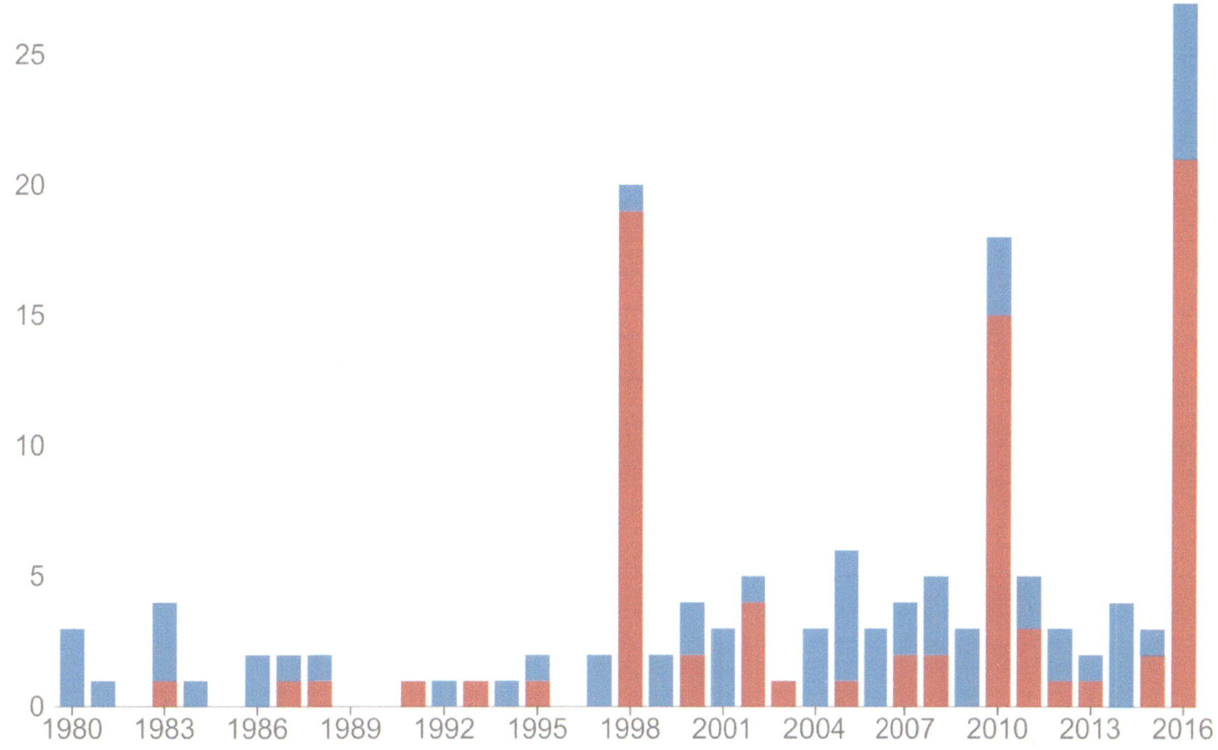

(a) Describe what the data is showing. 2

....

....

....

....

(b) Discuss which abiotic factors might be having an effect on coral reefs. 3

....

....

....

....

....

....

....

(c) The table below shows data on the number of Tuatara (reptiles endemic to New Zealand) in a population. 4

Construct a graph % males to year.

Year	Male Population	Female Population	Tuatara population	% Males	Ratio of Males to Females
1988	18	12	30	60	1.5
1989	20	16	36	56	1.25
1990	60	37	97	62	1.62
1991	53	39	92	58	1.36
1993	123	44	167	74	2.8
1994	126	61	187	67	2.07
1996	151	68	219	69	2.22
1997	154	72	226	68	2.14
1998	34	17	51	67	2
2000	227	132	359	63	1.72
2001	164	102	266	62	1.61
2005	120	43	163	74	2.79
2008	110	39	149	74	2.82
2010	101	33	134	75	3.06
2011	117	57	174	67	2.05

http://datanuggets.org/wp-content/uploads/2016/11/Tuatara-climate-change_StudentA.pdf

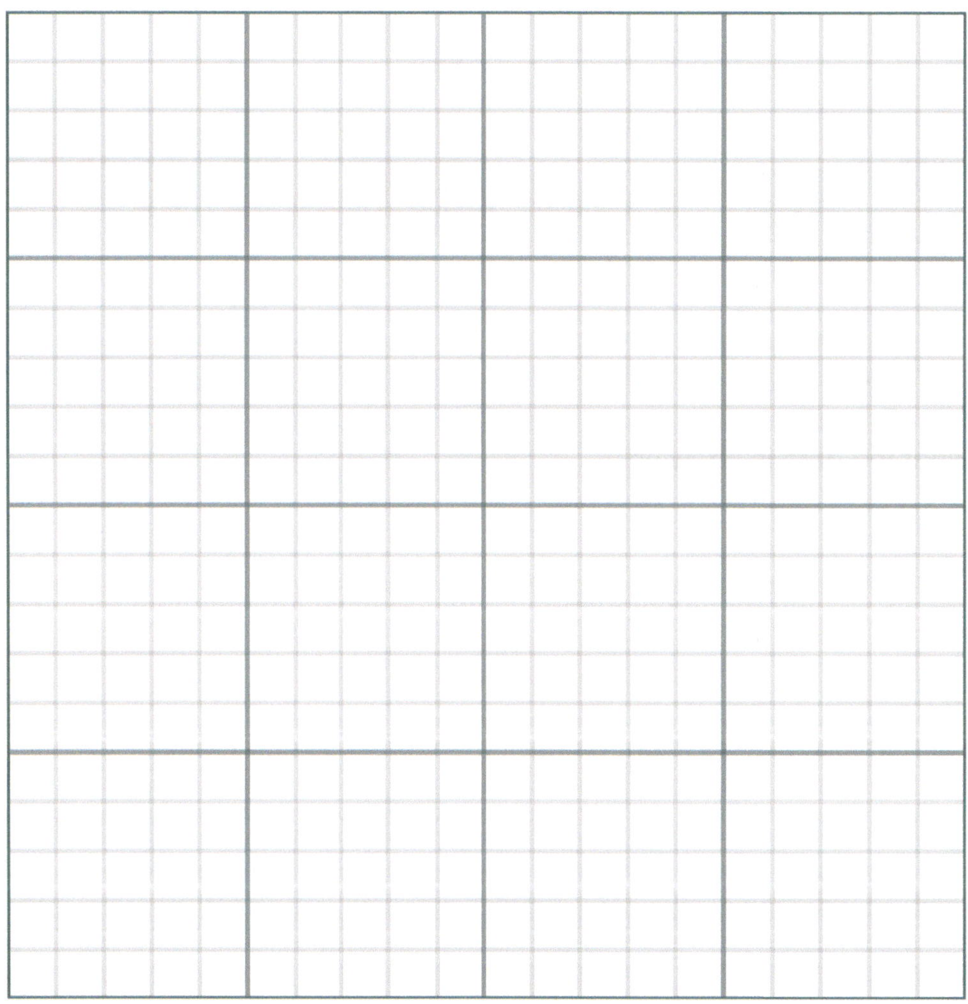

(d) The graph below shows the average temperature in the Tuatara ecosystem. 7

Discuss how both sets of data related to the Tuatara and coral bleaching are related, and assess how this shows the impact of humans on ecosystems.

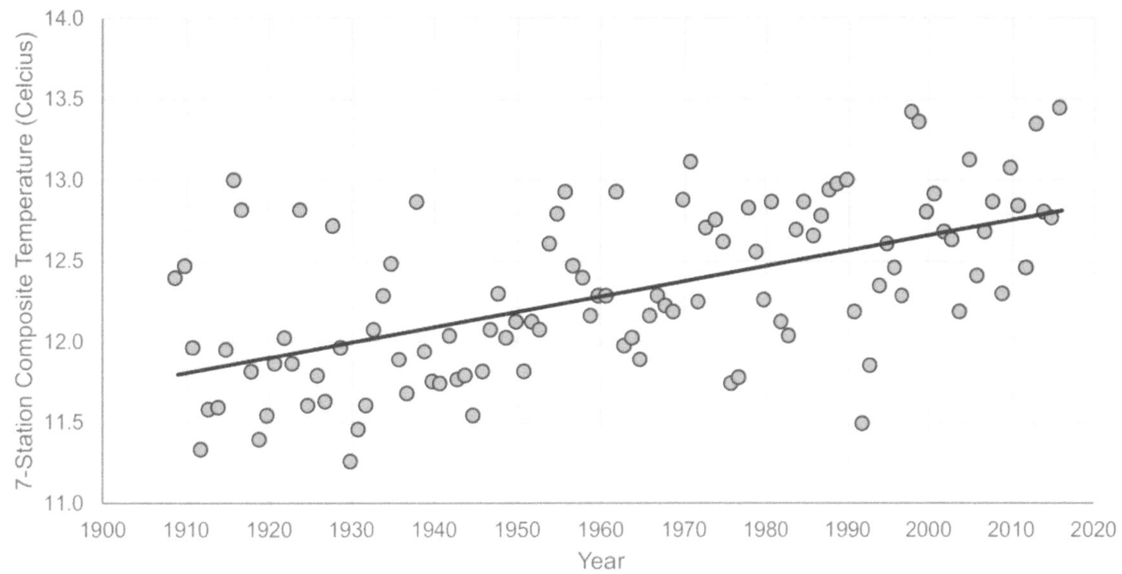

....

....

....

....

....

....

....

....

....

....

....

....

....

....

Marking Guidelines LMC
Biology Preliminary Examination 2022

Section I: Multiple-choice Answer Key

Question	**Answer**
1	A
2	C
3	C
4	D
5	A
6	B
7	A
8	B
9	C
10	B
11	A
12	D
13	C
14	B
15	D
16	D
17	A
18	C
19	D
20	B

Section II

Question 21 (a)

Criteria	Marks
• correctly names and labels a stomate	1

Sample answer:

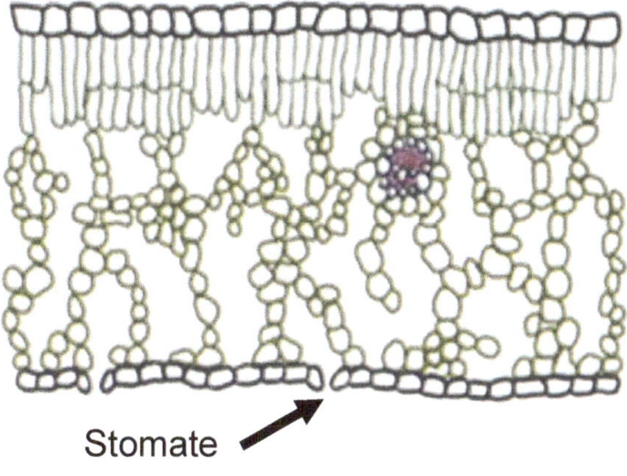

Question 21 (b)

Criteria	Marks
• Defines osmosis and outlines how it is involved in supplying water for photosynthesis	2
• Any relevant information	1

Sample answer:
Osmosis is the movement of water across a semipermeable membrane from an area of high water concentration to an area of lower water concentration. Water enters the root hairs of the plant by osmosis. The water travels up the xylem vessels to the leaf where it is used in photosynthesis.

Question 22

Criteria	Marks
• Describes the details of at least two adaptations	4
• Describes one adaption in detail **OR** • Outlines more than two adaptions	3
• Outlines two adaptions	2
• Any relevant information	1

Sample answer:
- Leaves have a thick cuticle to reduce transpiration loss
- Some may have wide or deep root systems to take advantage of any water in the soil

Question 23 (a)

Criteria	Marks
• Correctly identifies a reason	1

Sample answer:
So that both solutions were at the same starting temperature.

Question 23 (b)

Criteria	Marks
• A correct reason identified	2
• Any relevant information	1

Sample answer:
So that the rate of reaction could be observed and measured.

Question 23 (c)

Criteria	Marks
• Correctly describes a reason	2
• Any relevant information	1

Sample answer:
The experiment needs to be repeated a number of times with consistent results.

Question 23 (d)

Criteria	Marks
• Correctly explains a mechanism	2
• Any relevant information	1

Sample answer:
Amylase is an enzyme found in the mouth that breaks down carbohydrates into simple sugars. Amylase locks into the starch molecule and breaks it down into simple sugars.

Question 24 (a)

Criteria	Marks
• Identifies and explains the role of an organ in chemical digestion	2
• Any relevant information	1

Sample answer:
The liver produces bile. This helps digest lipids in the small intestine.

Question 24 (b)

Criteria	Marks
• Correctly contrasts the role of the organ in the two organisms • Uses correct scientific language	4
• Correctly contrasts the role of the organ in the two organisms	3
• Outlines the role of the organ in the two organisms	2
• Any relevant information	1

Sample answer:
Humans are omnivores, while rabbits are herbivores.

As one of the main functions of the liver is to digest lipids, and a plant based diet means that rabbits consume fewer foods with lipids in it, they do not require their bodies to produce large amounts of bile.

Question 25 (a)

Criteria	Marks
• Describes two reasons with supporting evidence	4
• Outlines one reason with supporting evidence **OR** • Describes one reason with evidence	3
• Outlines reasons	2
• Any relevant information	1

Question 25 (a) Sample answer:
As an invasive species, the cane toad has several characteristics that make it ideal for survival in Australia.

Firstly, it has no native predators on this continent; Australian predators have not adapted to the toxic venom they produce from glands on their shoulders. The cane toad also has a rapid reproductive cycle; females can breed at any time of the year and produce up to 30 000 eggs at a time.

Secondly, they have a broad, general diet and while better suited to moist conditions, can survive in drier areas, taking advantage of small patches of water or even the moisture from cow dung on stock trails.

Question 25 (b)

Criteria	Marks
• Identifies presence of cane toads as a negative selection pressure • Relates snake head size to ingestion of cane toads • Explains the change in snake population as evidence of evolution.	4
• Identifies presence of cane toads as a negative selection pressure • Relates snake head size to ingestion of cane toads • Outlines the change in snake population as evidence of evolution.	3
• Identifies presence of cane toads as a negative selection pressure • Relates snake head size to ingestion of cane toads	2
• Any relevant information	1

Sample answer:
In areas with cane toad infestation, red-bellied black snakes have faced a negative selection pressure due to the toxic toad venom. Snakes that are large enough to attempt to eat the toads usually die from ingesting the venom, and with their large head sizes often selected for larger, more venomous toads.

This has reduced the occurrence of these large-headed snakes in the population. What remains are the smaller-headed snakes; those that are either incapable of attempting to eat a cane toad or can only eat juvenile toads and are more likely to survive the smaller dose of venom.

This change in population is not evident in areas without cane toads, leading to the conclusion that black snake behaviour and physiology have evolved in response to the presence of toads.

Question 26

Criteria	Marks
• Correctly names and describes all the adaptations	5-6
• Correctly names and outlines all the adaptations	3-4
• Correctly names and outlines some of the adaptations	2
• Any relevant information	1

Sample answer:

Fat stored in the hump of a camel
Type of adaptation: Physiological
How this adaptation assists survival: Used as a source of energy, allowing them to go long periods without eating or drinking.

The platypus builds burrows near the water-edge
Type of adaptation: Behavioural
How this adaptation assists survival: To provide shelter, and regulate body temperature in both winter and summer. Also for nesting.

Plant on the lower canopy of the rainforest has wide, plate-like leaves
Type of adaptation: Structural
How this adaptation assists survival: Light is limited on the lower canopy and large, wide leaves that face upward have a large surface area to receive light for photosynthesis

Question 27

Criteria	Marks
• Explains using scientific language how enzymes work. • Explanation is clearly linked to the diagram with correct labelling or annotations	5-6
• Explains how enzymes work. • Explanation is linked to the diagram	3-4
• Outlines how enzymes work	2
• Any relevant information	1

Sample answer:

Enzymes are made from proteins and work when the pH, substrate concentration and temperature are optimal for that particular enzyme.

Enzymes have an active site that binds to a particular substrate when conditions are optimal.

When these conditions change, denaturation of the protein can occur.

Denaturation of the enzyme involves the destruction of the secondary (2) and tertiary (3) protein and Quaternary (4) structures. The primary structure (1) remains intact but the enzyme/substrate binding site is changed. The alpha helix and beta sheets in the protein uncoil into a random shape.

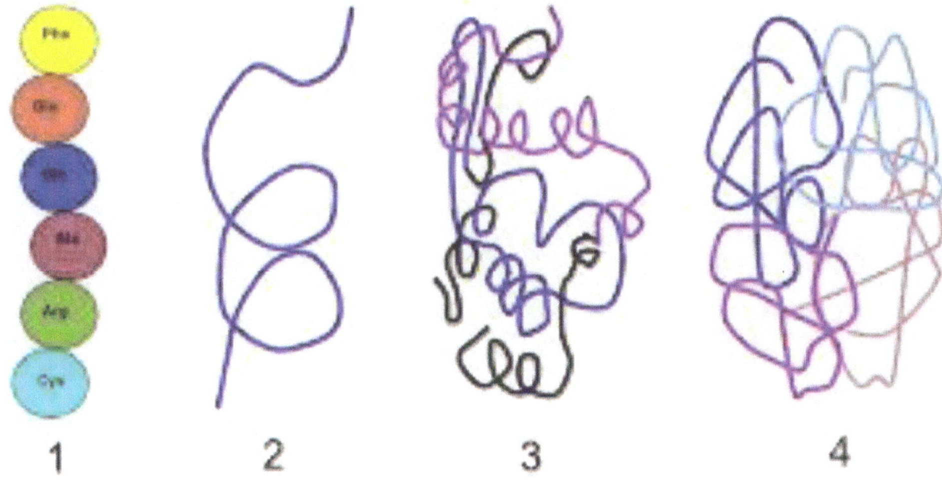

Question 28 (a)

Criteria	Marks
• Describes the data in the graph	2
• Any relevant information	1

Sample answer:

Since 1980 the number of coral bleaching events has increased. At the same time these events are becoming more severe.

Question 28 (b)

Criteria	Marks
• Describes at least two factors with detail	3
• Outlines two factors **OR** • Describes one factor in detail	2
• Any relevant information	1

Sample answer:
There may be many factors affecting the reefs.

- a rise in air and ocean temperatures that make it too hot for the reefs
- a rise in sea levels which restrict the light getting to the reefs
- a decrease in the pH of the ocean water affecting the organisms in the reef

Question 28 (c)

Criteria	Marks
• Correctly labeled axes • Correct data points and line	4
• Any 3 above	3
• Any 2 above	2
• Any relevant information	1

Sample answer:

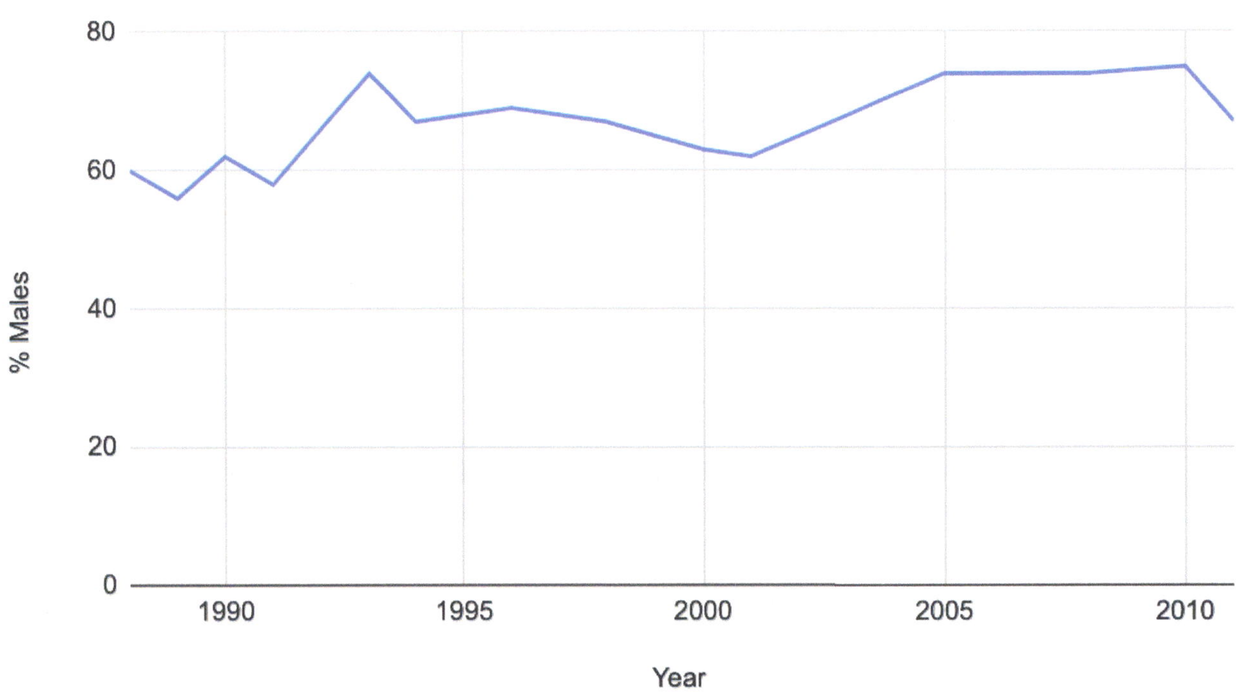

Question 28 (d)

Criteria	Marks
• Discussion relating both sets of data • Relates the data to human impacts • Makes a judgement related to both the Tuatara and coral, as well as organisms in general. • Clear and coherent	6-7
• Discussion relating both sets of data • Relates the data to human impacts	4-5
• Outlines both sets of data • Outlines human impacts	2-3
• Any relevant information	1

Sample answer:
The graph made from the supplied data shows that the percentage of males in the population is increasing. This may have a negative long-term impact on the population as the number of breeding females is reduced. This is confirmed by looking at the ratio of males to females compared to the total population. As the ratio increased, the total population decreased.

The graph of average temperatures shows an increase in average temperatures. The maximum temperature in each time-period in increasing. This increase is due to anthropogenic climate change caused by the burning of fossil fuels.

Taking both sets of data into account, it is possible to say that humans are negatively impacting the long-term viability of the Tuatara population. This may require direct human intervention in breeding to ensure the Tuatara's survival.

While this is obviously concerning for the tuatara, the data about coral bleaching suggests that this is an issue for many ecosystems.

In many cases organisms have unique biological niches, which only need very small abiotic changes to cause distress, and potentially extinction.

It is therefore imperative that humans attempt to mitigate the long-term affects of climate-change, and conserving in-danger organisms.

Mapping Grid

Section I

Q	Marks	Content	Syllabus Outcomes
1	1	M2 What is the difference in nutrient and gas requirements between autotrophs and heterotrophs?	BIO11-9
2	1	M1 What distinguishes one cell from another?	BIO11-8
3	1	M1 What distinguishes one cell from another?	BIO11-8
4	1	M3 How do environmental pressures promote a change in species diversity and abundance	BIO11-10
5	1	M3 What is the evidence that supports the Theory of Evolution by Natural Selection?	BIO11-10
6	1	M2 How are cells arranged in a multicellular organism?	BIO11-9
7	1	M3 What is the relationship between evolution and biodiversity?	BIO11-10
8	1	M3 How do adaptations increase the organism's ability to survive?	BIO11-10
9	1	M4 How do selection pressures within an ecosystem influence evolutionary change?	BIO11-11
10	1	M1 How do cells coordinate activities within their internal environment and the external environment?	BIO11-5, BIO11-8
11	1	M1 What distinguishes one cell from another?	BIO11-4, BIO11-8
12	1	M1 What distinguishes one cell from another?	BIO11-4, BIO11-8
13	1	M3 What is the evidence that supports the Theory of Evolution by Natural Selection?	BIO11-5, BIO11-10
14	1	M1 How do cells coordinate activities within their internal environment and the external environment?	BIO11-5, BIO11-8
15	1	M4 How do selection pressures within an ecosystem influence evolutionary change?	BIO11-6, BIO11-11
16	1	M4 What effect can one species have on the other species in a community?	BIO11-11
17	1	M1 How do cells coordinate activities within their internal environment and the external environment?	BIO11-5, BIO11-8
18	1	M1 How do cells coordinate activities within their internal environment and the external environment?	BIO11-4, BIO11-8

Q	Marks	Content	Syllabus Outcomes
19	1	M4 What effect can one species have on the other species in a community?	BIO11-11
20	1	M2 How does the composition of the transport medium change as it moves around an organism?	BIO11-9

Section II

Q	Marks	Content	Syllabus Outcomes
21 (a)	1	M1 How do cells coordinate activities within their internal environment and the external environment? M2 How does the composition of the transport medium change as it moves around an organism?	BIO11-8, BIO11-9
21 (b)	2	M1 How do cells coordinate activities within their internal environment and the external environment? M2 What is the difference in nutrient and gas requirements between autotrophs and heterotrophs?	BIO11-8, BIO11-9
22	4	M4 How do selection pressures within an ecosystem influence evolutionary change?	BIO11-11
23 (a)	1	M2 What is the difference in nutrient and gas requirements between autotrophs and heterotrophs?	BIO11-9
23 (b)	1	M2 What is the difference in nutrient and gas requirements between autotrophs and heterotrophs?	BIO11-9
23 (c)	2	M2 What is the difference in nutrient and gas requirements between autotrophs and heterotrophs?	BIO11-2, BIO11-3, BIO11-5, BIO11-9
23 (d)	2	M2 What is the difference in nutrient and gas requirements between autotrophs and heterotrophs?	BIO11-9
24 (a)	2	M2 What is the difference in nutrient and gas requirements between autotrophs and heterotrophs?	BIO11-9
24 (b)	4	M2 What is the difference in nutrient and gas requirements between autotrophs and heterotrophs?	BIO11-4, BIO11-9
25 (a)	4	M3 How do environmental pressures promote a change in species diversity and abundance?	BIO11-6, BIO11-10
25 (b)	4	M3 How do environmental pressures promote a change in species diversity and abundance?	BIO11-6, BIO11-10
26	6	M3 How do adaptations increase the organism's ability to survive?	BIO11-7, BIO11-10

Q	Marks	Content	Syllabus Outcomes
27	6	M1 How do cells coordinate activities within their internal environment and the external environment?	BIO11-7, BIO11-8
28 (a)	2	M4 What effect can one species have on the other species in a community?	BIO11-11
28 (b)	3	M3 How do environmental pressures promote a change in species diversity and abundance? M4 How do selection pressures within an ecosystem influence evolutionary change?	BIO11-4, BIO11-5, BIO11-10, BIO11-11
28 (c)	4	M4 How do selection pressures within an ecosystem influence evolutionary change?	BIO11-4, BIO11-5, BIO11-11
28 (c)	7	M3 What is the relationship between evolution and biodiversity? M4 How can human activity impact on an ecosystem?	BIO11-6, BIO11-7, BIO11-10, BIO11-11

2022 TRIAL HIGHER SCHOOL CERTIFICATE EXAMINATION	
Biology	
General Instructions	• Reading time – 5 minutes • Working time – 3 hours • Write using black pen • Draw diagrams using pencil • Calculators approved by NESA may be used
Total marks: 100	Section I – 20 marks (pages 2–7) • Attempt Questions 1–20 • Allow about 35 minutes for this section
	Section II – 80 marks (pages 8–25) • Attempt Questions 21–35 • Allow about 2 hours and 25 minutes for this section

Section I

20 marks
Attempt Questions 1–20
Allow about 35 minutes for this section

Use the multiple-choice answer sheet for Questions 1–20.

1. The cells responsible for the adaptive immune response are B lymphocytes (B Cells) and T lymphocytes (T Cells). Some B lymphocytes develop into

   A. antigens which stimulate an immune response.
   B. plasma cells which produce antibodies against the pathogen.
   C. cytokines which aid with the coordination of the immune response.
   D. cytotoxic cells which seek out and destroy infected cells.

2. A student walking home on a summer day starts to sweat. Sweating is what part of a negative feedback loop?

   A. Stimulus
   B. Response
   C. Receptor
   D. Effector

3. The following pedigree shows the pattern of inheritance of a genetic disorder caused by a mutation. The inheritance pattern confirms this disorder is caused by what sort of mutation?

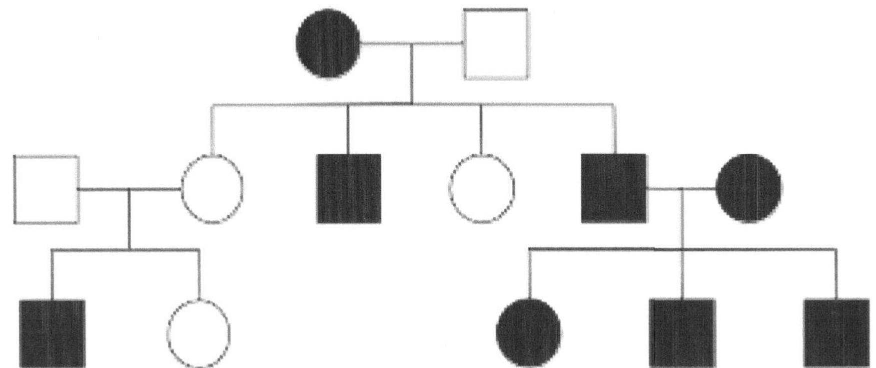

   A. Chromosomal mutation
   B. Germline mutation
   C. Somatic mutation
   D. Spontaneous mutation

4. What process involves the formation of a new individual cell from a mother cell?

   A. Regeneration
   B. Budding
   C. Sexual reproduction
   D. Parthenogenesis

5. Using the information on the graph on hormones during pregnancy, which hormone is an indicator that an embryo is ready for implantation in the endometrium?

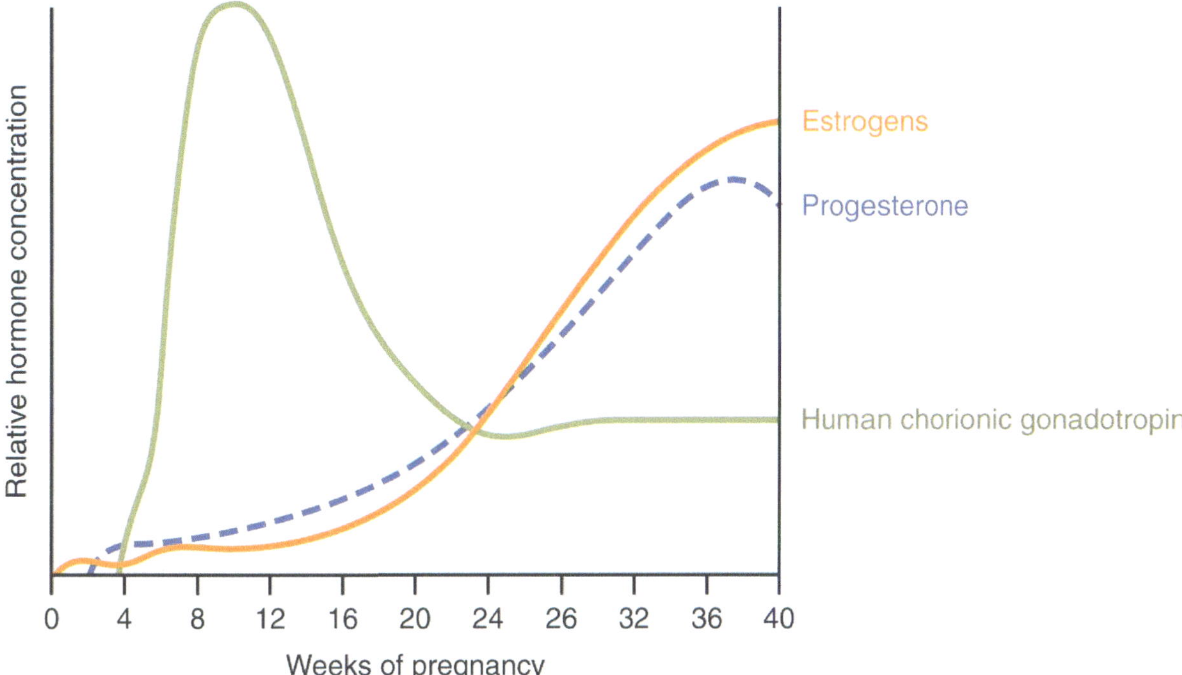

   A. Oestrogen
   B. Progesterone
   C. Testosterone
   D. Human Chorionic gonadotropin

6. A patient has conductive hearing loss caused by abnormal bone growth. Which technology would be ineffective in assisting them with their hearing loss?

   A. Hearing aids
   B. One conduction implants
   C. Cochlear implants
   D. Surgery

7. How does vaccination prevent infectious disease?

   A. Vaccines stimulate specific antibodies to be produced.
   B. Vaccines prevent antigens from stimulating an immune response.
   C. Vaccines reduce a pathogen's capacity to survive outside the body.
   D. Vaccines decrease the body's inflammatory response.

8. The following data table details the 10 leading causes of death in Australia for males, in 2019, as recorded by the Australian Institute for Health and Welfare . What can be concluded from this data?

Deaths in Australia (males, 2019)

Rank	Cause of death	Number	Per cent
1	Coronary heart disease	10,448	12.1
2	Dementia including Alzheimer disease	5,397	6.2
3	Lung cancer	5,139	5.9
4	Cerebrovascular disease	4,047	4.7
5	Chronic obstructive pulmonary disease	3,901	4.5
6	Prostate cancer	3,582	4.1
7	Colorectal cancer	2,856	3.3
8	Diabetes	2,700	3.1
9	Suicide	2,502	2.9
10	Influenza and pneumonia	1,775	2

Source: AIHW National Mortality Database.

   A. More males died from heart disease than females in 2019.
   B. There were 10448 cases of coronary heart disease in Australia in 2019
   C. Infectious diseases represented a smaller percentage of the top ten causes of deaths in Australian males than non-infectious causes in 2019.
   D. Infectious diseases represented a majority of the top ten causes of deaths in Australian males in 2019.

9. The mRNA strand differs in one nitrogenous base pair.
   Which base is different on the mRNA strand?

   A) Guanine
   B) Thymine
   C) Cytosine
   D) Adenine

10. Tay-Sachs disease is caused when a child inherits a recessive allele from both parents that prevents the enzyme hexosaminidase A being produced. This is an example of a/an:

A. Genetic disease
B. Nutritional disease
C. Environmental disease
D. Cancer

11. What would be used to cut short sections of DNA for DNA profiling?

A. DNA polymerase
B. Pepsin
C. Restriction enzymes
D. Micro-scissors

12. Sometimes during DNA replication, a point mutation occurs where a single nitrogenous base is replaced by another nitrogenous base. This type of mutation is said to be a:

A. Insertion
B. Substitution
C. Deletion
D. Frame shift

13. Identify which of the following are non-cellular pathogens.

A. Bacteria and protozoa
B. Bacteria and fungi
C. Virus and protozoa
D. Virus and prion

14. Identify the type of mutation that occurred.

Original: ATC GCC TGA
New: ATG GCC TGA

A. Frameshift
B. Substitution
C. Insertion
D. Deletion

15. Passive, natural immunity occurs by

  A. Previous exposure to a disease.
  B. Antivenom injected after a snake bite.
  C. Baby receiving antibodies from a mothers breast milk.
  D. Vaccination.

16. Varicella (commonly referred to as chickenpox) can be a serious disease that affects adults and children. It is very contagious. Varicella is quite contagious. It is easily spreadable through families, schools and daycare centres. When an infected person coughs or sneezes, virus particles are inhaled and spread. It can also be spread by coming into contact with the fluid from another person's chickenpox blisters. Vaccination is the most effective strategy to prevent the spread of varicella.

  Which of the following modes of transmission identifies the way varicella is spread?

  A. Vector
  B. Direct contact
  C. Indirect contact
  D. Direct and indirect contact

17. Aboriginal Australians have a rich and detailed knowledge of native Australian Plants. Scientists are now discovering that many bioactive compounds found in plants are effective antimicrobial agents. An experiment was conducted to determine the effectiveness of three Australian plant extracts against the bacteria *Bacillus subtilis*. The results are shown below.

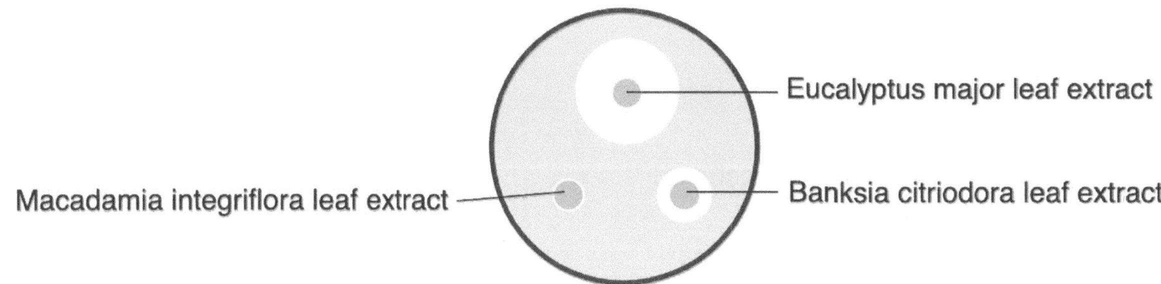

  Which of the following conclusions can be drawn from the results.

  A. *Eucalyptus major* leaf extract and *banksia citriodora* leaf extract contain antibiotic compounds that are effective against Bacillus subtilis.
  B. *Eucalyptus major* leaf extract and *banksia citriodora* leaf extract contain antifungal compounds that are effective against Bacillus subtilis.
  C. *Macadamia integrifolia* leaf extract contains antibiotic compounds but they are not effective against *Bacillus subtilis*.
  D. *Macadamia integrifolia* leaf extract contains antifungal compounds but they are not effective against *Bacillus subtilis*.

18. Which of the following adaptations assist the bilby with temperature regulation in dry, arid parts of Australia?

A. Migrating to the north in winter
B. Small, thick ears
C. Low surface area to volume ratio
D. Nocturnal feeding activity

19. mRNA codes are read

A. 3 prime to 5 prime
B. 5 prime to 3 prime
C. In any direction
D. They are never read

20.

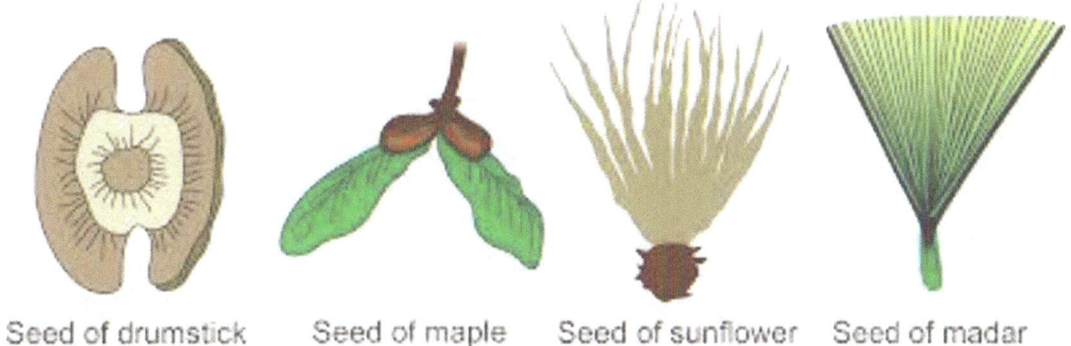

What type of plant seed dispersal is shown in the images above?

A. Animal
B. Water
C. Wind
D. Self Pollination

2022 TRIAL HIGHER SCHOOL CERTIFICATE EXAMINATION

Biology

Section II Answer Booklet

Centre Number

Student Number

80 marks
Attempt Questions 21–35
Allow about 2 hours and 25 minutes for this section

Instructions	• Write your Centre Number and Student Number at the top of this page • Answer the questions in the spaces provided. These spaces provide guidance for the expected length of response. • Show all relevant working in questions involving calculations.

Please turn over

Question 21 (4 marks)

The following data was collected on the effectiveness of the Australian Government's *Sun Smart* campaign which was developed and published in the late 1980s. Respondents were asked if they regularly used at least one sun protection strategy (eg. sunscreen, wearing a hat) and if they had been affected by sunburn at least once that year.

This survey was conducted every year at the same location, over a 40 year period, before results were collated and averaged for each decade.

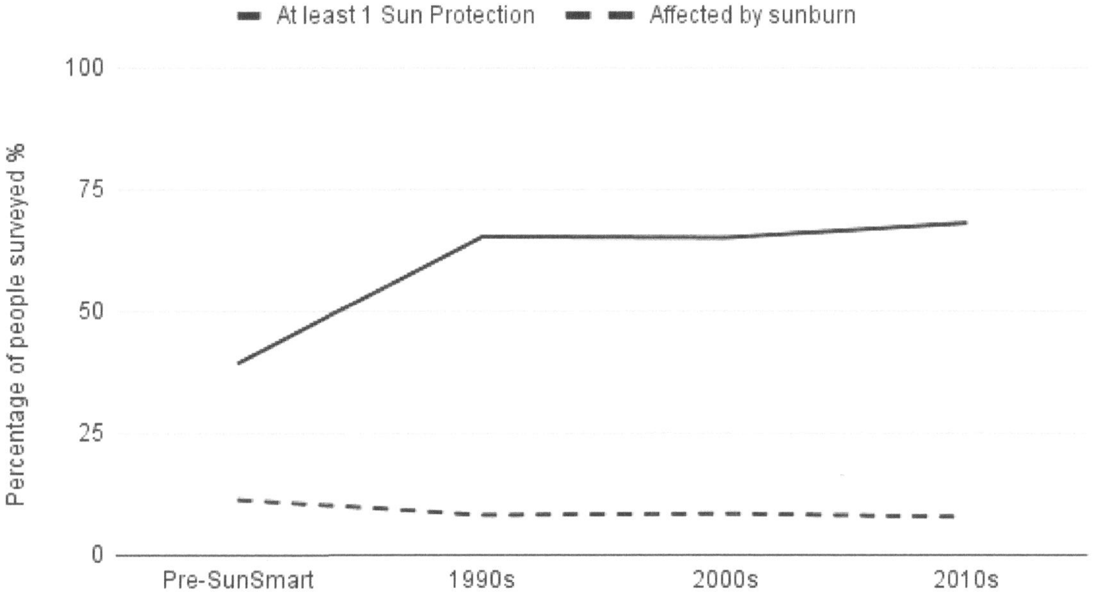

A local newspaper made the following statement after publishing the graph: "*The Sun Smart campaign improved habits of sun protection in Australians, and reduced the risk of skin damage*".

Analyse the data in the graph to assess the validity of this statement.

....

....

....

....

....

....

....

....

Question 22 (3 marks)

Protein consists of one or more polypeptide chains. It can be folded into specific shapes to carry out a specific function.

Explain how a protein is made from the DNA molecule and its importance to an organism.

....

....

....

....

....

....

Question 23 (4 marks)

Describe how artificial insemination can alter the genetic composition of a population.

....

....

....

....

....

....

....

....

Question 24 (6 marks)

(a) Injuries to body tissues cause the release of chemicals that trigger an inflammatory response. Identify TWO chemicals that are released in tissues and can trigger an inflammatory response. 2

....
....
....
....

(b) Draw a flowchart to outline what happens in the inflammatory response. 4

Question 25 (5 marks)

(a) A patient presents to an eye clinic, complaining that they are having trouble reading the board at university and can't see very well while driving, especially at night. The doctor suspects they have a type of vision impairment. 3

Draw a labelled diagram of the eye of this patient, identifying their suspected condition and indicating the focal point of light in relation to the retina.

....

....

....

....

....

....

(b) The doctor prescribes corrective lenses for the patient. Draw a new diagram showing the lens and how it has corrected the focal point in this patient's eye. 2

....

....

....

....

Question 26 (10 marks)

(a) Use the statements in the word bank to fill in the empty boxes in the diagram below to complete the negative feedback loop outlining the role of antidiuretic hormone (ADH) in osmoregulation. 3

Lower volume of more concentrated urine	Less water is reabsorbed by the kidney	Blood water content low
Pituitary reduce the amount of ADH produced	Higher amount of water reabsorbed by the kidney	Excess sweating or water loss

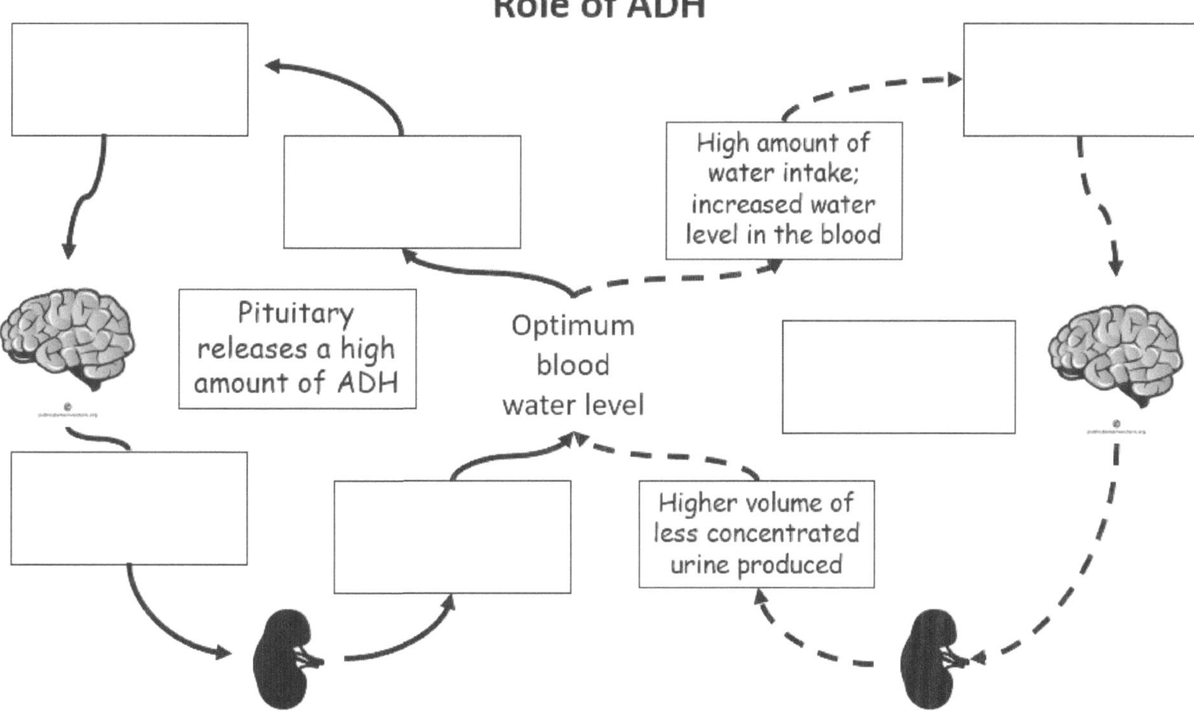

(b) A student's blood glucose levels were measured every hour for 12 hours, from 7am until 7pm. 5

Use the data in the table to draw a line graph.

Time of Day	Blood glucose levels (mmol/L)
07:00	4.2
08:00	6.1
09:00	4.7
10:00	4.2
11:00	3.8
12:00	3.8
13:00	6.2
14:00	4.1
15:00	3.8
16:00	3.8
17:00	4.0
18:00	6.0
19:00	4.8
20:00	4.0

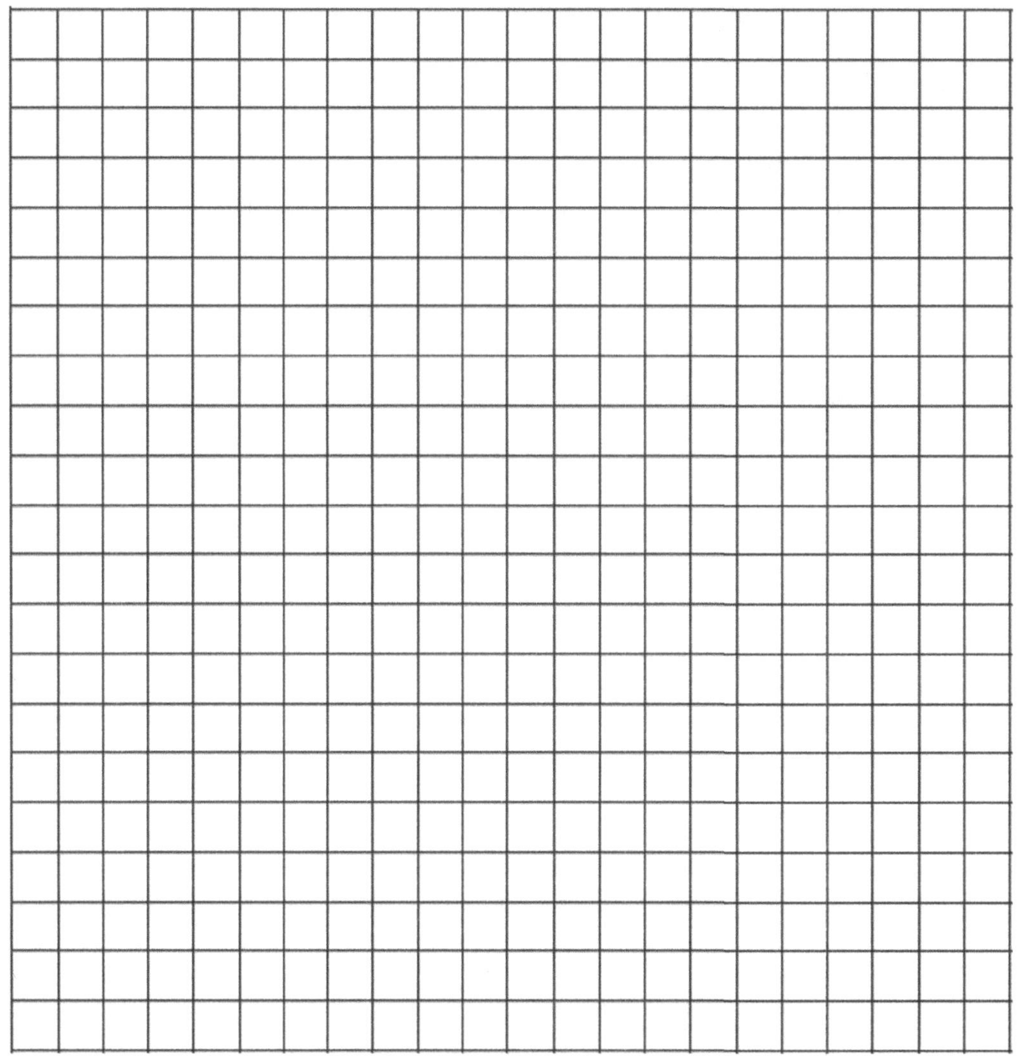

(c) Using your graph, suggest the times at which the student ate throughout the day. 2

....
....
....
....

Question 27 (3 marks)

Complete the table below.

Pathogen	Distinguishing characteristics of the pathogen	Disease caused by the pathogen
Virus		
Bacteria		
Protozoan		

Question 28 (4 marks)

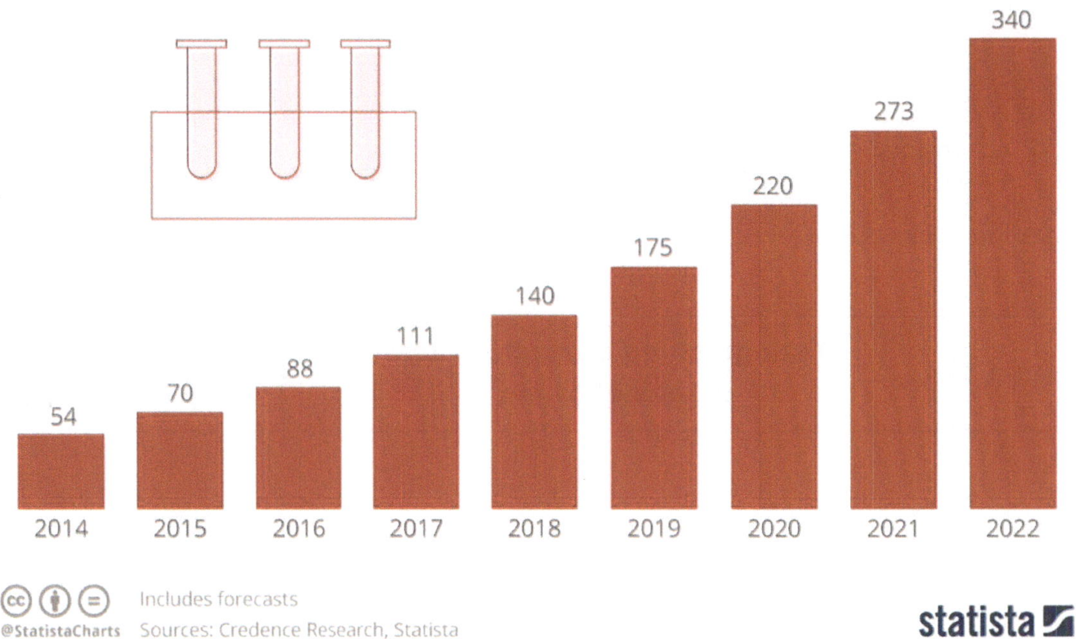

(a) Genetic testing kits like Ancestry DNA are genetic testing kits that use DNA samples, such as saliva, to track a person's ancestry, find family members and disclose possible health risks. 2
What are the possible social risks associated with at home genetic testing kits?

....

....

....

....

(b) Why do you think genetic testing is growing in popularity and what is the likely future trend? 2

....

....

....

....

Question 29 (3 marks)

How do scientists know that the DNA molecule is in a 3D Double Helical structure? 3

....
....
....
....
....
....

Question 30 (7 marks)

Cardiovascular Disease (CVD) is a general term for conditions affecting the heart or blood vessels. It's usually associated with a build-up of fatty deposits inside the arteries.

Cardiovascular diseases cause 27% of deaths in Australia.

The diagram below is a Pedigree chart on a family with a bloodline of CVD.

- The circles represent females and squares males
- Those coloured black have CVD
- CVD is represented by the letter 'd'

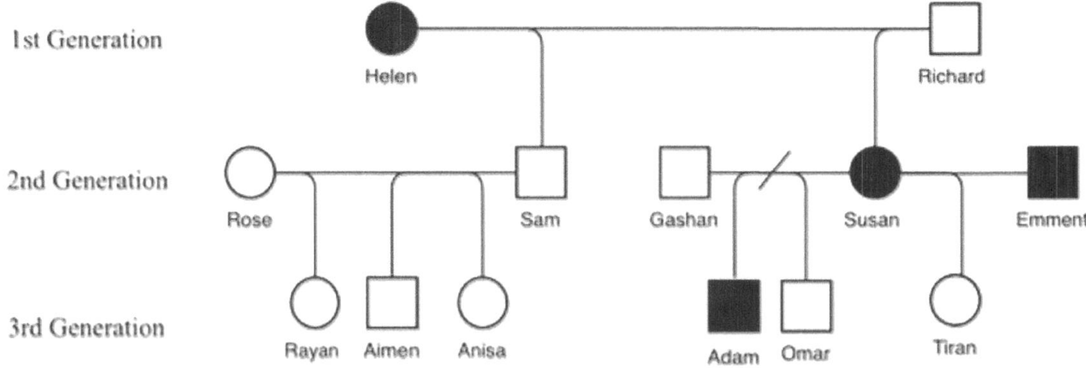

(a) What is a pedigree and how is it used to explain genetic inheritance? 2

....

....

....

....

....

....

(b) What is the genotype and phenotype of Emment? 2

....

....

....

....

(c) Determine the possible genotypes and phenotype of Anisa. Explain your answer. 3

....

....

....

....

....

....

Question 31 (5 marks)

Evaluate the effectiveness of disease prevention/management options for a named non-infectious disease. 5

....
....
....
....
....
....
....
....
....
....

Question 32 (7 marks)

The graph and table below show data describing the COVID-19 pandemic.

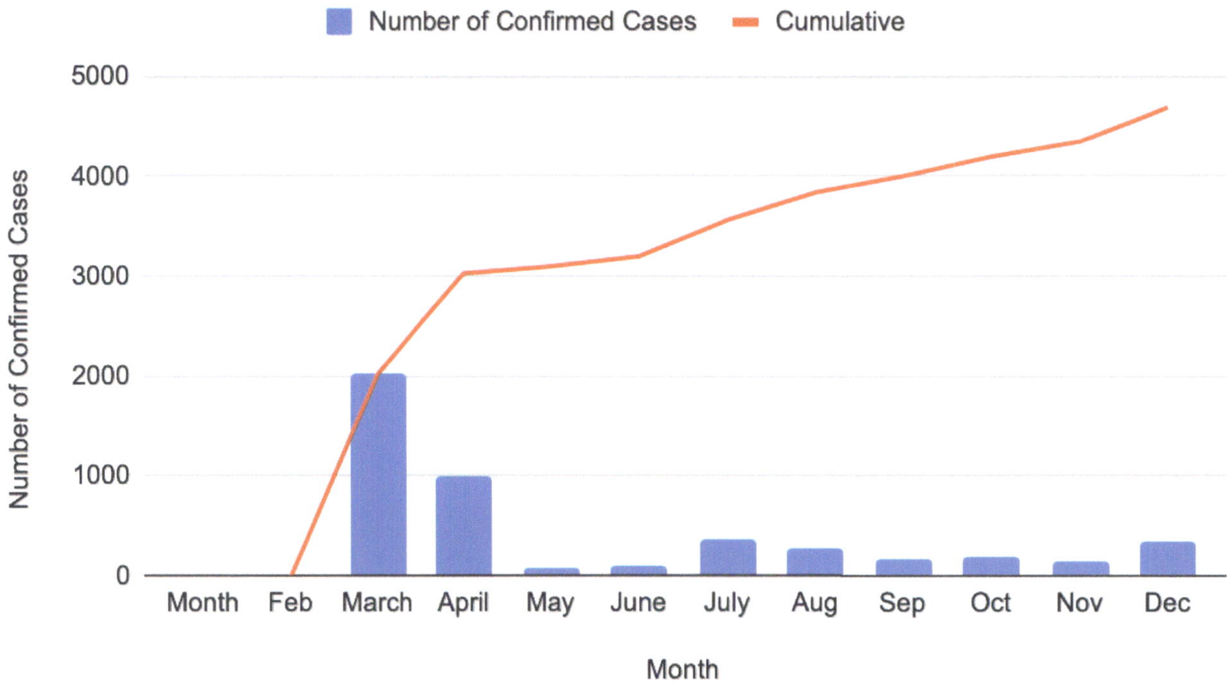

NSW COVID Vaccination Rate - Updated March 2022

NSW COVID Vaccination Rate	Total (Ages 16 and over)	Total (Ages 12-15)	Total (Ages 5-11)
All providers - first dose	95.8%	83.6%	47.9%
All providers - second dose	94.4%	79.0%	1.7%
All providers - third dose	55.8%	X	X

(a) What is the trend for the confirmed cases for COVID-19 in NSW, in 2020 and state one possible reason for this trend. 2

....
....
....
....

(b) Since early 2021 there were 2 main vaccinations available to NSW residents: Pfizer and AstraZeneca. Mid 2021 the Moderna vaccination also became available. **2**

The roll out began in February 2021 and was based around risk of exposure. NSW residents were encouraged to get 2 doses of a COVID-19 vaccination. Currently booster vaccinations are also being offered to NSW residents aged 16 and over.

Explain the importance of booster vaccinations.

....
....
....
....

(c) With reference to the above data and information, discuss the role of public health campaigns in keeping people safe during the COVID-19 pandemic. **3**

....
....
....
....
....
....

Question 33 (6 marks)

(a) Explain why there is controversy about the use of recombinant DNA technology and the development of transgenic species **3**

....
....
....
....
....
....

(b) Pose advantages and disadvantages of this type of technology. **3**

....
....
....
....
....
....

Question 34 (9 marks)

Louis Pasteur was a French chemist, biologist and microbiologist who contributed to our understanding of the spread of infectious disease. He conducted a famous experiment using a swan necked flask which is shown below.

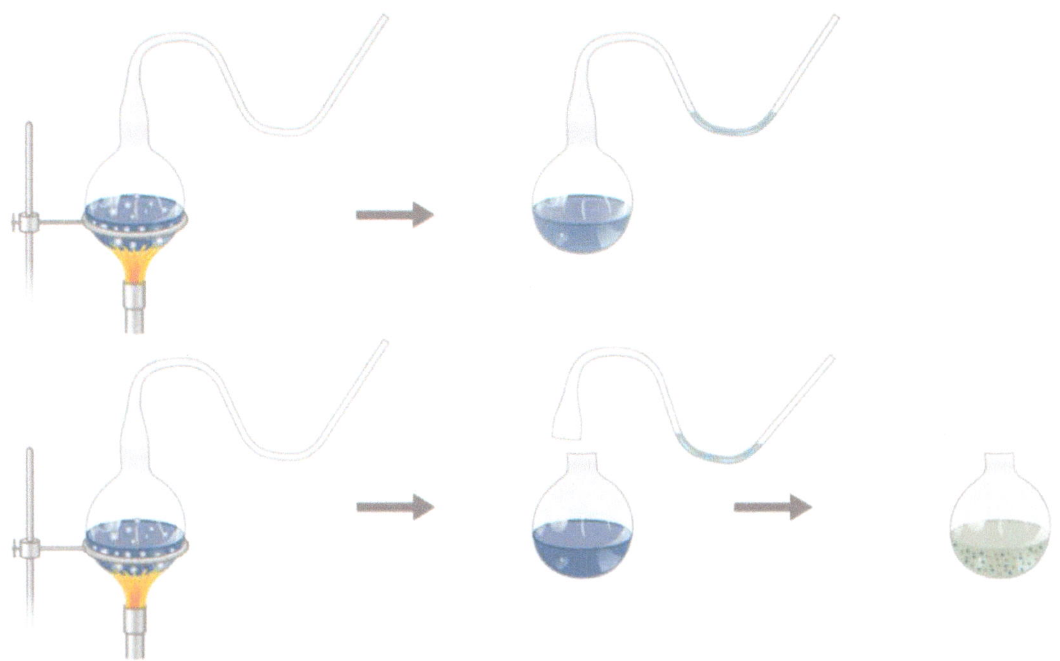

(a) Complete the following table to identify the variables in Pasteur's experiment. 3

Independent Variable	Dependent Variable	Controlled Variable

(b) Outline a valid procedure for this experiment. 2

....

....

....

....

(c) Explain why Pasteur's experiment using swan necked flasks provided evidence against the theory of spontaneous generation and aided in the acceptance of the germ theory. 4

....
....
....
....
....
....
....
....

Question 35 (4 marks)

Outline how quarantine has prevented the spread of a disease into Australia. 4

....
....
....
....
....
....
....
....

End of Paper

Marking Guidelines

Section I: Multiple-choice Answer Key

Question	Answer
1	B
2	B
3	B
4	B
5	D
6	C
7	A
8	C
9	B
10	A
11	C
12	B
13	D
14	B
15	D
16	D
17	A
18	D
19	B
20	C

Section II

Question 21

Criteria	Mark
• Refers explicitly to the stimulus to provide reasons for or against the validity of the statement. • Refers to trends in the data • Demonstrates an understanding of key features of valid epidemiological studies, such as controlling variables, error/bias and reliability.	4
• Makes reference to the data and the methods of the study • Provides a reason for or against the validity of the statement	3
• Makes reference to the data or the methods of the study	2
• Some information relevant to the data provided	1

Suggested answer:
While the data suggests an increase in sun protection habits over time and a slight decrease in rates of sunburn, we cannot make that statement conclusively from this study alone. The method of collecting only self-identifying data from survey respondents could impact on the validity of the results by introducing bias. There are other variables that have not been considered, such as other causes of skin damage other than sunburn. We also do not know how many people were surveyed, and it was only in one location, so we cannot reliably conclude that the habits of all Australians have been changed.

Question 22

Criteria	Marks
• Explain how a DNA molecule is transcribed then translated into the needed protein. Explains protein synthesis and its importance to a living organism.	3
• Explains DNA transcription and translation. Necessary to have amino acid subunits to make protein	2
• Explains DNA as a molecule to make proteins	1

Question 22 suggested answer:
Enzymes read the information from the DNA molecule and transcribe it into a molecule called mRNA. Then, the information in the mRNA molecule is translated using a tRNA molecule into the language of amino acids, which are the building blocks of protein. The amino acids are strung together and released when a stop codon is present. The length of amino acids form the specific protein required. The protein folds into the tertiary or quaternary shape needed for the specific substrate.

Question 23

Criteria	Marks
• Relates the use of artificial insemination to favourable genetics. • Provides an example of favourable genetics. • Clearly describes how AI alters the genetic composition of an organism. • Identifies that AI can have a negative impact on genetic diversity.	4
• Relates the use of artificial insemination to favourable genetics. • Provides an example of favourable genetics. • Describes how AI alters the genetic composition of an organism. • Identifies that AI can have a negative impact on genetic diversity.	3
• Relates the use of artificial insemination to favourable genetics. • Provides an example of favourable genetics. • Attempts to describe how AI alters the genetic composition of an organism.	2
• • Some relevant information.	1

Suggested answer:
AI is a common practice in agriculture to ensure favourable traits become more common in stock.

In cattle used in beef production, male animals with a higher amount of muscle will have their semen extracted and used to inseminate breeding stock. This will increase the chance of the next generation producing a higher muscle to body mass ratio.

After successive generations the stock will have more muscle. At a genetic level more of the animals will have genes that express increased growth of muscle.

However, this can also have a negative impact if those genes being expressed are susceptible to diseases. In plant agriculture the desire for uniform fruit and vegetables has meant that many plant species have almost identical genomes meaning that any infection can run the risk of destroying the entire population, such as extinct species of bananas.

Question 24 (a)

Criteria	Marks
• Correctly identifies two chemicals that are released in tissues and can trigger an inflammatory response.	2
• Correctly identifies one chemical that is released in tissues and can trigger an inflammatory response.	1

Suggested answer:
Histamines and Prostaglandins

Question 24 (b)

Criteria	Marks
• Draws a flowchart that clearly shows the sequence involved in the inflammatory response.	4
• Draws a substantially correct flow chart.	3
• Shows some steps in the inflammatory response.	2
• Provides some relevant information.	1

Suggested answer:

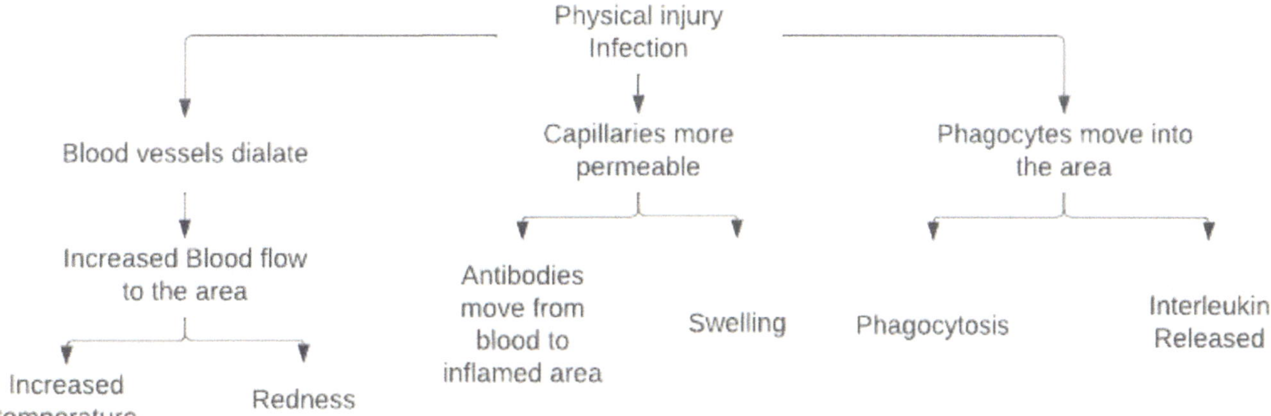

Question 25 (a)

Criteria	Mark
• Correctly identifies the condition as myopia • Draws a diagram correctly depicting the focal point in front of the retina • Drawing is labelled	3
• Correctly identifies the condition as myopia AND • Draws the focal point correctly OR labels the drawing	2
• Myopia is identified OR correctly identifies the focal point but unlabelled	1

Suggested answer:

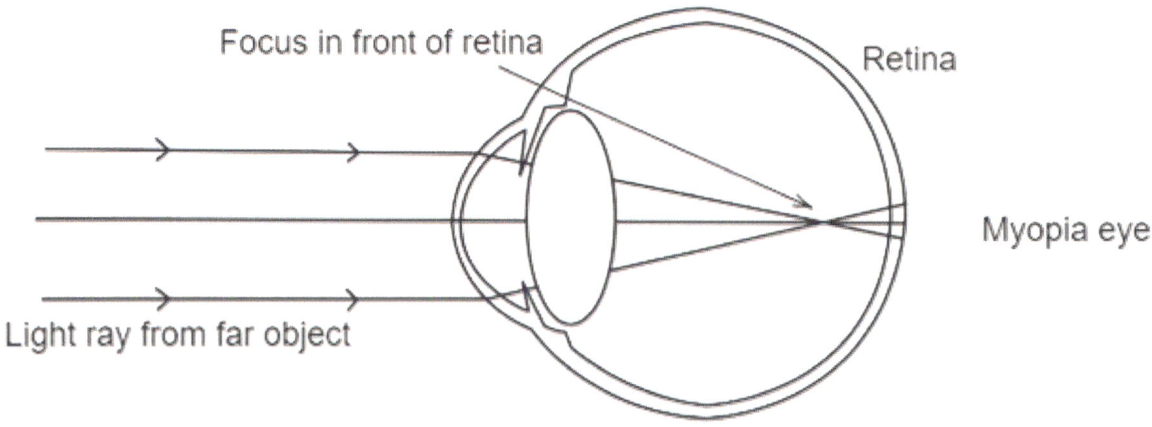

Question 25 (b)

Criteria	Marks
• Draws a concave lens AND corrects the focal point	2
• Draws an attempt at a lens AND/OR corrects the focal point	1

Suggested answer:

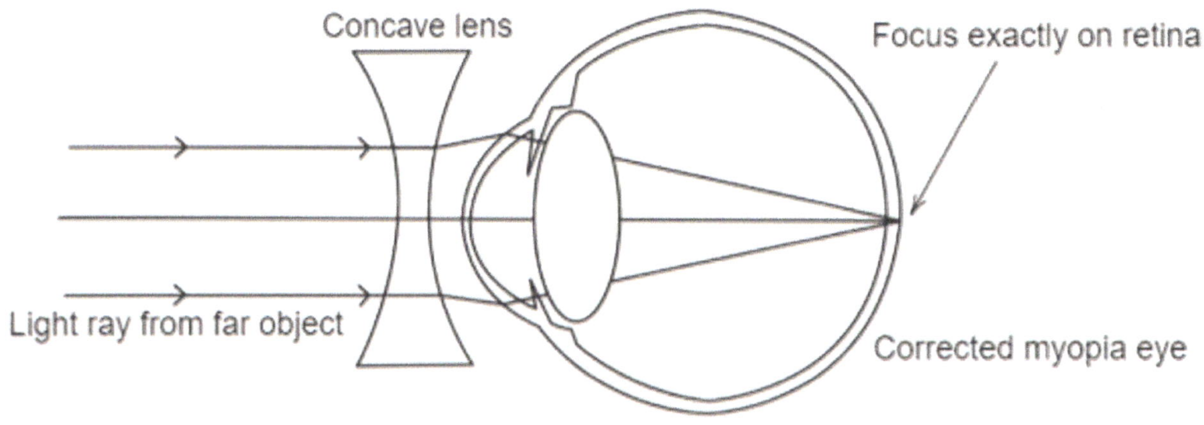

Question 26 (a)

Criteria	Marks
• All parts of the flow chart are correctly identified	3
• Four parts of the flow chart are correctly identified	2
• Two parts of the flow chart are correctly identified	1

Suggested answer:

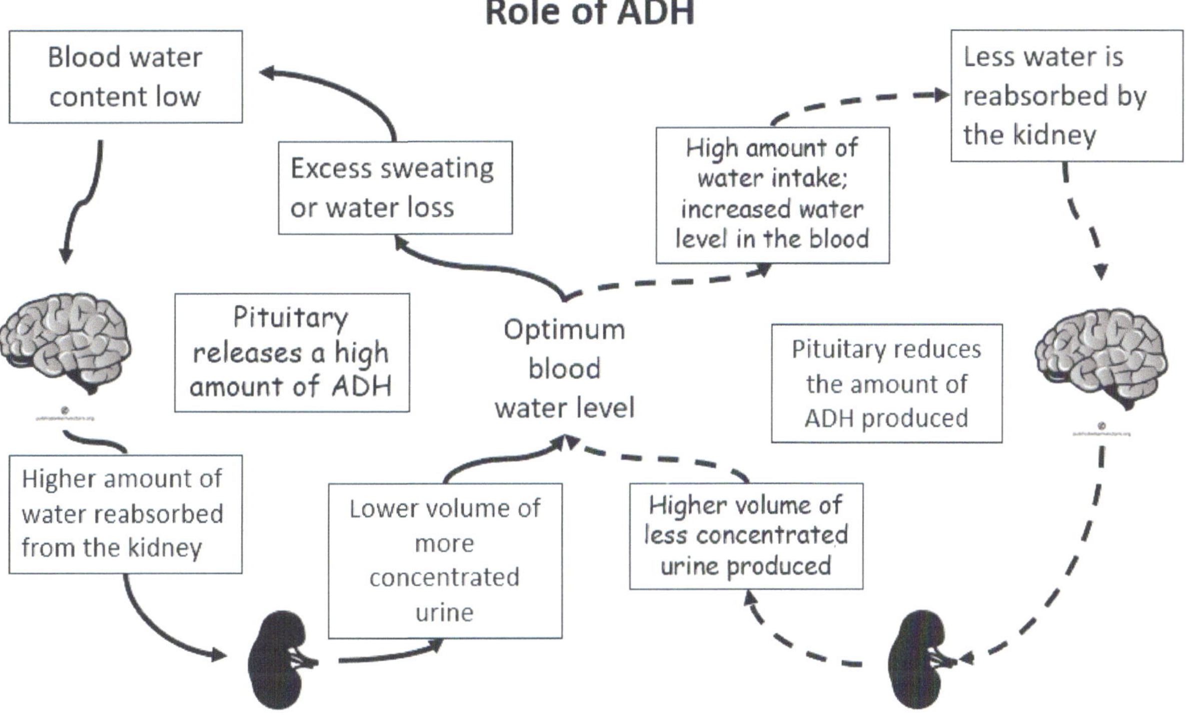

Question 26 (b)

Criteria	Marks
• Correctly labelled axis • Correct and appropriate scale • Correct plotting of a line graph • Appropriate title	5
• Any of the 4 above	4
• Any of the 3 above	3
• Any of the 2 above	2
• Any of the above	1

Suggested answer:

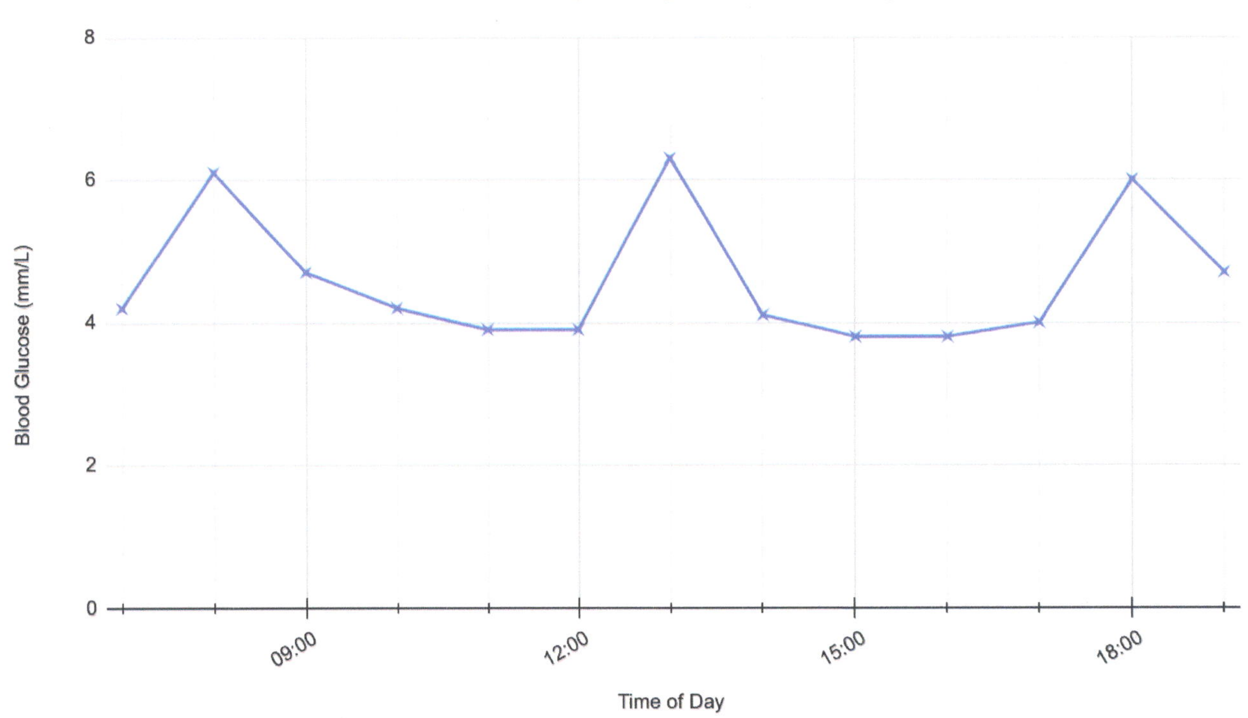

Question 26 (c)

Criteria	Marks
• Correctly identifies the three times	2
• Identifies at least 1 correct time	1

Suggested answer:

On 3 occasions: Between 7am-8am, 12-1pm, 5pm-6pm

Question 27

Criteria	Marks
• Provides a correct distinguishing characteristic for each pathogen • Provides a correct disease caused by each pathogen	3
• Provides a correct distinguishing characteristic for TWO pathogens • Provides a correct disease caused by TWO pathogens	2
• • Provides some relevant information	1

Suggested answer:
Students may have different characteristics or examples

Pathogen	Distinguishing characteristics of the pathogen	Disease caused by the pathogen
Virus	• Non cellular • Contain genetic material • Able to invade living cells and reproduce	HIV
Fungi	• Living • Eukaryotic • Some are unicellular, most are multicellular	Tinea
Protozoan	• Living • Unicellular • Eukaryotic • Visible with light microscope	Malaria

Question 28 (a)

Criteria	Marks
• Two risk clearly identified	2
• One risk identified	1

Suggested answer:
Issues with identity theft and knowledge Companies abusing data collected and sharing with stakeholders and others, emotional distress, cultural expectations, Controversy over how these companies and government keep the data, cost of kits limits access to all individuals.

Question 28 (b)

Criteria	Marks
• A clear reason and trend identified	2
• A reason or trend identified	1

Suggested answer:
Genetic testing is growing in popularity due to advancement in biotechnology and gene therapy, increased accessibility through the internet, ease of delivery to customers, increase awareness through social media exposure and marketing.

Question 29

Criteria	Mark
• Extensively explains the history behind the DNA molecule using Rosalind Franklin x-ray diffraction experiment	3
• Outlines the history behind the DNA molecule using Rosalind Franklin x-ray diffraction experiment	2
• Any relevant information	1

Suggested answer:
Rosalind Franklin used X-Ray diffraction images of DNA which showed it was a helical structure. It was found to contain a sugar phosphate backbone with the nitrogenous bases forming a rung inside the tightly spiralled structure. The bases are held together by hydrogen bonds and by forces between the stacked bases.

The backbone of sugar phosphates are antiparallel and form a 3 prime and 5 prime end. The DNA molecule is tightly packed so as to protect the delicate nitrogenous bases from damage. It is important that the DNA molecule is tightly packed as a 3D double helix so that the long strands of DNA can be packed into the small nucleus of the cell.

Question 30 (a)

Criteria	Mark
• Defines the term pedigree and its use in genetic inheritance	2
• Either gives defines pedigree and its use in genetic inheritance	1

Suggested answer:
A pedigree is a graphical representation of the ancestry of living organisms. It helps assist in the study of inheritance of genes of a family over time.

Question 30 (b)

Criteria	Marks
• Correctly identifies the genotype and phenotype of individual	2
• Correctly identifies the genotype OR phenotype of individual	1

Suggested answer:
dd, and has CVD

Question 30 (c)

Criteria	Marks
• Discusses the possible genotype and phenotype of Anisa	3
• States the genotype and phenotype of Anisa	2
• Any relevant information	1

Suggested answer:
Anisa does not exhibit signs of the condition. However, one of her grandparents, Helen, did.

Anisa's father, Sam, showed no signs of CVD, and would have been heterozygous for CVD

Depending on which genes she received from her father, Anisa can either be homozygous DD and have no CVD gene or heterozygous Dd and be a carrier for CVD.

Question 31

Criteria	Mark
• Identifies a non-infectious disease • Discusses specific strategies for prevention and/or management of the disease • Links the prevention/treatment options to their effect on mortality/prevalence rates • Provides data/evidence to support the evaluation of effectiveness	5
• Identifies a non-infectious disease • Discusses at least one specific strategy for prevention and/or management of the disease • Links the prevention/treatment options to their effect on mortality/prevalence rates	4
• Identifies a non-infectious disease • Describes a strategy used for the prevention or management of the disease • Attempts to link the strategy with its effectiveness	3
• Identifies a non-infectious disease • Identifies a strategy for prevention or management of that disease	2
• Any relevant information	1

Suggested answer:

Both public education campaigns and newer technologies such as genetic screening play a role in the prevention and management of breast cancer. Educational programs and campaigns inform the public about the symptoms and risk factors of breast cancer, as well as advertising ways to seek diagnosis and treatment early and easily. Free breast cancer screening is provided to women over the age of 50 in NSW and is made accessible with 'buses' that travel to convenient locations around the state. Genetic screening allows for early detection by testing patients for the BRCA1 and BRCA2 genes. These genetic tests allow for a more accurate assessment of a patient's risk of developing breast cancer in the future, and better informs their treatment options.

The improved access to diagnosis means that breast cancer is still the most common cancer in Australia, however, the mortality rate for breast cancer has dropped significantly since the 1970s thanks to early treatment and diagnosis.

Question 32 (a)

Criteria	Mark
• Gives the downward trend and states one possible reason	2
• Any relevant information	1

Suggested answer:
From the graph, there is a decrease in the number of COVID 19 cases. This can be due to the increase in the number of people in the population getting the vaccine.

Question 32 (b)

Criteria	Mark
• Explains the importance of booster shots	2
• Any relevant information	1

Suggested answer:
A booster shot triggers the immune system to attack the foreign microorganism, as if it is the real pathogen.

This helps your immune system "remember" the disease-causing organism. If the individual is exposed to the microorganism again, the antibodies can recognise and kill it before it causes harm.

Research has shown that booster shots train your body to recognise the virus or bacteria and defend itself. Depending on the type of vaccine and the manufacturer, you might get a booster shot weeks, months, or even years after your first shot.

Question 32 (c)

Criteria	Mark
• Discusses the role of public health campaigns by referring to the given information	3
• States the role of public health campaigns by referring to some of the given information	2
• Any relevant information	1

Question 32 (c) suggested answer:

The role of a public health campaign is to inform people about possible health dangers dues to infections such as COVID-19.

This might involve running target advertisements encouraging people to socially distance and wear facemasks.

The graph shows that after an initial increase in case numbers, the case numbers plateaued, suggesting that government interventions probably had a positive effect on public health.

The table shows vaccination rates. The high number, above 94%, suggests that people followed the health advice and received their vaccinations.

Other possible discussion points.

- Facts sheets about symptoms of COVID -19
- Staying away from people with COVID-19
- Wearing PPE-signage and videos
- Testing centres (PCR) and Rapid Antigen Test (RAT)
- Wash your hands, sanitisers, deep cleaning
- Covid-19 training, regular refresher training on infection prevention and control measures.
- Front line workers
- Quarantine and isolation
- Limit public movement (5 km rule for Local Government Areas (LGA) with high transmission rates

Question 33 (a)

Criteria	Mark
• Discusses the technology with specific examples • Describes any controversial aspects of the technology	3
• Outlines the technology • States a controversial aspect of the technology	2
• • Any relevant information	1

Suggested answer:

The introduction of transgenic species raises ethical issues related to environmental concerns as well as animal welfare, human safety concerns and confidentiality issues.
When a transgenic organism is released into the environment, how will it affect the food web and the organisms in the gene pool? Will their modified genetic ability cause harm to the naturally occurring organisms?

(Suggested answer continues onto next page)

Question 33 (a) suggested answer – continued:
Will genetically modified food affect the organisms that consume it or use it?

The advantages of transgenic species are that they provide food supply in the form of livestock and agricultural food to feed an increasing world population.

Transgenic produce can be altered so that it lasts a long time unrefrigerated and gives it a longer shelf life. For example, tomatoes.

The use of bacterial plasmids to make insulin for human use for diabetics. Insulin can easily be produced, extracted and purified and reduce rejection by the user.

Question 33 (b)

Criteria	Mark
• Discusses the advantages and disadvantages of the technology	3
• Outlines some advantages or disadvantages of the technology	2
• Any relevant information	1

Suggested answer:
The introduction of transgenic species raises ethical issues related to environmental concerns as well as animal welfare, human safety concerns and confidentiality issues.
When a transgenic organism is released into the environment, how will it affect the food web and the organisms in the gene pool? Will their modified genetic ability cause harm to the naturally occurring organisms?

Will genetically modified food affect the organisms that consume it or use it.
The advantages of transgenic species are that they provide food supply in the form of livestock and agricultural food to feed an increasing world population.

Transgenic produce can be altered so that it lasts a long time unrefrigerated and gives it a longer shelf life. For example, tomatoes.
The use of bacterial plasmids to make insulin for human use for diabetics. Insulin can easily be produced, extracted and purified and reduce rejection by the user.

Question 34 (a)

Criteria	Mark
• Correctly identifies the independent, dependent and a controlled variable.	3
• Correctly identifies two variables.	2
• Correctly identifies one variable.	1

Suggested answer:

Independent Variable	Dependent Variable	Controlled Variable
Shape of the neck of the flask	Presence of microbial growth of the broth	Various e.g. - Type of broth - Length of time boiled - Amount of broth - Size of flask - Method of boiling

Question 34 (b)

Criteria	Mark
• Outlines a valid procedure that describes the experiment.	2
• Any relevant information	1

Suggested answer:

First nutrient broth was prepared. Then equal amounts of the broth were placed into two swan necked flasks. Next, the broth was boiled in order to kill any living matter in the liquid. One flask was left with the bent "S" shape. While the other had the swan neck broken off. The sterile broths were left to sit at room temperature. The results were observed over a period of weeks.

Question 34 (c)

Criteria	Mark
• States the theory of spontaneous generation. • Describes the results of the experiment. • Explains the relationship between the experiment results and the two theories.	4
• Describes the results of the experiment. • Explains the relationship between the experiment results and the two theories.	3
• Describes the results of the experiment. • Explains the relationship between the experiment results and one of the theories.	2
• Any relevant information	1

Suggested answer:
The results of this experiment show that microbial growth was only present in the flask that was open to air. The theory of spontaneous generation stated that life could appear from non-living matter. If this was the case, there would be microbial growth present in both of the flasks. Therefore, this experiment aided the acceptance of the germ theory by showing that pathogens were transmitted through the air and they did not spontaneously generate.

Question 35

Criteria	Mark
• Describes a quarantine method that prevents the spread of a disease into Australia. • Identifies an example of a disease. • Describes how this disease impacts the organism infected. • Outline the impact this disease would have on Australia if it entered the country.	4
• Describes a quarantine method that prevents the spread of a disease into Australia. • Identifies an example of a disease. • Outline the impact this disease would have on Australia if it entered the country.	3
• Describes a quarantine method that prevents the spread of a disease into Australia. • Identifies an example of a disease.	2
• Any relevant information	1

Suggested answer:
Biosecurity Australia inspects goods and organisms that are brought into and out of Australia. American serpentine leafminer is an example of a plant disease that can pose a serious threat to our agricultural industry. Tiny maggots burrow between the layers of the leaves of vegetables and soft leaved plants. When they mine between these layers it causes damage to the plant. Therefore, this is considered a plant pest. Biosecurity Australia ensures that Australia is protected against various diseases like this that could impact our agricultural industry, ecosystems and quality of life.